GPT-4

FOR

DEVELOPERS

GPT-4

FOR

DEVELOPERS

Oswald Campesato

MERCURY LEARNING AND INFORMATION
Boston, Massachusetts

Publisher: David Pallai
MERCURY LEARNING AND INFORMATION
121 High Street, 3rd Floor
Boston, MA 02110
info@merclearning.com
www.merclearning.com
800-232-0223

O. Campesato. *GPT-4 for Developers.*
ISBN: 978-150152-248-2

Library of Congress Control Number: 2023950028
232425321   This book is printed on acid-free paper in the United States of America.

Our titles are available for adoption, license, or bulk purchase by institutions, corporations, etc. For additional information, please contact the Customer Service Dept. at 800-232-0223 (toll free).

All of our titles are available in digital format at academiccourseware.com and other digital vendors. Companion files (figures and code listings) for this title are available by contacting *info@merclearning.com.* The sole obligation of MERCURY LEARNING AND INFORMATION to the purchaser is to replace the files, based on defective materials or faulty workmanship, but not based on the operation or functionality of the product.

I'd like to dedicate this book to my parents – may this bring joy and happiness into their lives.

CONTENTS

Preface   *xiii*

Chapter 1: ChatGPT and GPT-4   **1**

What is Generative AI?   1
    Key Features of Generative AI   1
    Popular Techniques in Generative AI   2
    What Makes Generative AI Different   2
Conversational AI Versus Generative AI   3
    Primary Objectives   3
    Applications   3
    Technologies Used   3
    Training and Interaction   4
    Evaluation   4
    Data Requirements   4
Is DALL-E Part of Generative AI?   4
Are ChatGPT-3 and GPT-4 Part of Generative AI?   5
DeepMind   6
    DeepMind and Games   6
    Player of Games (PoG)   6
OpenAI   7
Cohere   8
Hugging Face   8
    Hugging Face Libraries   8
    Hugging Face Model Hub   8
AI21   9
InflectionAI   9
Anthropic   9
What is Prompt Engineering?   10
    Prompts and Completions   10
    Types of Prompts   11

Instruction Prompts   11
Reverse Prompts   11
System Prompts Versus Agent Prompts   12
Prompt Templates   12
Prompts for Different LLMs   13
Poorly Worded Prompts   14
What is ChatGPT?   15
ChatGPT: GPT-3 "on Steroids?"   16
ChatGPT: Google "Code Red"   16
ChatGPT Versus Google Search   17
ChatGPT Custom Instructions   17
ChatGPT on Mobile Devices and Browsers   18
ChatGPT and Prompts   18
GPTBot   18
ChatGPT Playground   19
ChatGPT and Medical Diagnosis   19
Plugins, Advanced Data Analysis, and Code Whisperer   20
Plugins   20
Advanced Data Analysis   21
Advanced Data Analysis Versus Claude 2   22
Code Whisperer   22
Detecting Generated Text   23
Concerns About ChatGPT   23
Code Generation and Dangerous Topics   24
ChatGPT Strengths and Weaknesses   24
Sample Queries and Responses from ChatGPT   25
Alternatives to ChatGPT   27
Google Bard   27
YouChat   28
Pi from Inflection   28
Machine Learning and ChatGPT: Advanced Data Analysis   28
What is InstructGPT?   29
VizGPT and Data Visualization   30
What is GPT-4?   31
GPT-4 and Test-Taking Scores   32
GPT-4 Parameters   32
GPT-4 Fine-Tuning   32
ChatGPT and GPT-4 Competitors   33
Bard   33
CoPilot (OpenAI/Microsoft)   34
Codex (OpenAI)   35
Apple GPT   35
PaLM-2   35
Med-PaLM M   35
Claude 2   36

LlaMa-2	36
How to Download LlaMa-2	36
LlaMa-2 Architecture Features	37
Fine-Tuning LlaMa-2	37
When is GPT-5 Available?	38
Summary	39

Chapter 2: ChatGPT and Python **41**

Simple Calculator	42
Simple File Handling	43
Simple Web Scraping	43
Basic Chatbot	44
Basic Data Visualization	45
Basic Pandas	46
Generate Random Data	47
Recursion: Fibonacci Numbers	48
Object Oriented Programming	49
Asynchronous Programming with asyncio	49
Working with Requests in Python	53
Image Processing with PIL	54
Exception Handling	57
Generators in Python	57
Roll 7 or 11 with Two Dice	58
Roll 7 or 11 with Three Dice	59
Roll 7 or 11 with Four Dice	61
Mean and Standard Deviation	62
Summary	62

Chapter 3: ChatGPT and Data Visualization **65**

Working with Charts and Graphs	65
Bar Charts	66
Pie Charts	66
Line Graphs	67
Heat Maps	67
Histograms	67
Box Plots	68
Pareto Charts	68
Radar Charts	68
Treemaps	69
Waterfall Charts	69
Line Plots with Matplotlib	69
A Pie Chart Using Matplotlib	70
Box-and-Whisker Plots using Matplotlib	71
Time Series Visualization with Matplotlib	72
Stacked Bar Charts with Matplotlib	73

Donut Charts Using Matplotlib 75
3D Surface Plots with Matplotlib 75
Radial or Spider Charts with Matplotlib 77
Matplotlib's Contour Plots 79
Stream Plots for Vector Fields 80
Quiver Plots for Vector Fields 82
Polar Plots 83
Bar Charts with Seaborn 83
Scatter Plots with Regression Lines Using Seaborn 84
Heatmaps for a Correlation Matrix with Seaborn 85
Histograms with Seaborn 86
Violin Plots with Seaborn 87
Pair Plots Using Seaborn 88
Facet Grids with Seaborn 89
Hierarchical Clustering 90
Swarm Plots 91
Joint Plots for Bivariate Data 92
Point Plots for Factorized Views 93
Seaborn's KDE Plots for Density Estimations 94
Seaborn's Ridge Plots 95
Summary 96

Chapter 4: Linear Regression With GPT-4 **97**
What is Linear Regression? 98
Examples of Linear Regression 98
Metrics for Linear Regression 99
Coefficient of Determination (R^2) 100
Linear Regression with Random Data with GPT-4 101
Linear Regression with a Dataset with GPT-4 104
Describe the Features of the death.csv Dataset 105
The Preparation Process of the Dataset 107
The Exploratory Analysis 109
Detailed EDA on the death.csv Dataset 110
Bivariate and Multivariate Analyses 113
The Model Selection Process 115
Code for Linear Regression with the death.csv Dataset 117
Describe the Model Diagnostics 119
Additional Model Diagnostics 121
More Recommendations from GPT-4 122
Summary 124

Chapter 5: Visualization with Generative AI **125**
Generative AI and Art and Copyrights 126
Generative AI and GANs 126
GANs (Generative Adversarial Networks) 127

What is Diffusion?   127
   Diffusion Image Sample   128
   Diffusion Models Versus GANs   129
   What are Diffusers and DDPMs?   129
CLIP (OpenAI)   130
GLIDE (OpenAI)   131
Text-to-Image Generation   131
   Stability AI/Stable Diffusion   132
   Imagen (Google)   133
   Make-a-Scene (Meta)   133
   Diffuse the Rest   133
   GauGAN2 (NVIDIA)   135
   PromptBase   135
   Limitations of Text-to-Image Models   135
Text-to-Image Models   135
The DALL-E Models   137
   DALL-E   137
   DALL-E 3   137
   Paid Accounts for DALL-E   138
   Invoking the DALL-E API   139
DALL-E 2   142
   DALL-E 2 Overview   142
   The DALL-E 2 Model   143
   DALL-E 2 Content Preparation   144
   DALL-E-Bot   144
DALL-E Demos   145
Text-to-Video Generation   146
   Meta (Make-a-Video)   146
   Imagen Text-to-Video   146
   Ruben Villegas and Google (Phenaki)   147
Text-to-Speech Generation   147
   Whisper (OpenAI)   148
Summary   148

Index   *149*

PREFACE

WHAT IS THE VALUE PROPOSITION FOR THIS BOOK?

This book contains an assortment of Python 3.x code samples that were generated by ChatGPT and GPT-4. Chapter 1 provides an overview of ChatGPT and GPT-4, followed by Chapter 2 that contains Python 3.x code samples for solving various programming tasks in Python 3.x. Chapter 3 contains Python code samples for data visualization, and Chapter 4 contains code samples for linear regression. The final chapter covers visualization with Gen AI (aka Generative AI).

THE TARGET AUDIENCE

This resource is designed to bridge the gap between theoretical understanding and practical application, making it a useful tool for software developers, data scientists, AI researchers, and tech enthusiasts interested in harnessing the power of GPT-4 in Python environments.

DO I NEED TO LEARN THE THEORY PORTIONS OF THIS BOOK?

The answer depends on the extent to which you plan to become involved in working with ChatGPT and Python, perhaps involving LLMs and generative AI. In general, it's probably worthwhile to learn the more theoretical aspects of LLMs that are discussed in this book.

GETTING THE MOST FROM THIS BOOK

Some people learn well from prose, others learn well from sample code (and lots of it), which means that there's no single style that can be used for everyone.

Moreover, some programmers want to run the code first, see what it does, and then return to the code to delve into the details (and others use the opposite approach).

Consequently, there are various types of code samples in this book: some are short, and some are long.

WHAT DO I NEED TO KNOW FOR THIS BOOK?

Although this book is introductory in nature, some knowledge of Python 3.x with certainly be helpful for the code samples. Knowledge of other programming languages (such as Java) can also be helpful because of the exposure to programming concepts and constructs. The less technical knowledge that you have, the more diligence will be required in order to understand the various topics that are covered.

If you want to be sure that you can grasp the material in this book, glance through some of the code samples to get an idea of how much is familiar to you and how much is new for you.

DOES THIS BOOK CONTAIN PRODUCTION-LEVEL CODE SAMPLES?

This book contains basic code samples that are written in Python, and their primary purpose is to familiarize you with basic Python to help you understand the Python code generated via ChatGPT. Moreover, clarity has higher priority than writing more compact code that is more difficult to understand (and possibly more prone to bugs). If you decide to use any of the code in this book, you ought to subject that code to the same rigorous analysis as the other parts of your code base.

WHAT ARE THE NON-TECHNICAL PREREQUISITES FOR THIS BOOK?

Although the answer to this question is more difficult to quantify, it's very important to have a desire to learn about NLP, along with the motivation and discipline to read and understand the code samples. As a reminder, even simple APIs can be a challenge to understand them the first time you encounter them, so be prepared to read the code samples several times.

HOW DO I SET UP A COMMAND SHELL?

If you are a Mac user, there are three ways to do so. The first method is to use Finder to navigate to Applications > Utilities and then double click on the Utilities application. Next, if you already have a command shell available, you can launch a new command shell by typing the following command:

```
open /Applications/Utilities/Terminal.app
```

A second method for Mac users is to open a new command shell on a MacBook from a command shell that is already visible simply by clicking command+n in that command shell, and your Mac will launch another command shell.

If you are a PC user, you can install Cygwin (open source *https://cygwin.com/*) that simulates bash commands, or use another toolkit such as MKS (a commercial product). Please read the online documentation that describes the download and installation process. Note that custom aliases are not automatically set if they are defined in a file other than the main start-up file (such as .bash_login).

COMPANION FILES

All the code samples and figures in this book may be obtained by writing to the publisher at *info@merclearning.com*.

WHAT ARE THE "NEXT STEPS" AFTER FINISHING THIS BOOK?

The answer to this question varies widely, mainly because the answer depends heavily on your objectives. If you are interested primarily in NLP, then you can learn about other LLMs (large language models).

If you are primarily interested in machine learning, there are some subfields of machine learning, such as deep learning and reinforcement learning (and deep reinforcement learning) that might appeal to you. Fortunately, there are many resources available, and you can perform an Internet search for those resources. One other point: the aspects of machine learning for you to learn depend on who you are: the needs of a machine learning engineer, data scientist, manager, student or software developer are all different.

O. Campesato
December 2023

## CHAPTER 1

CHATGPT AND GPT-4

This chapter contains information about the main features of ChatGPT and GPT-4, as well as some of their competitors. We start with information generated by ChatGPT regarding the nature of generative AI, and then discuss the differences between conversational AI versus generative AI. According to ChatGPT, ChatGPT itself, GPT-4, and DALL-E are included in generative AI. This chapter also discusses alternatives to ChatGPT. Finally, we will discuss some of the features of GPT-4 that power ChatGPT. You will also learn about some competitors of GPT-4, such as Llama-2 (Meta) and Bard (Google).

WHAT IS GENERATIVE AI?

Generative AI refers to a subset of artificial intelligence models and techniques designed to generate new data samples that are similar in nature to a given set of input data. The goal is to produce content or data that was not part of the original training set but is coherent, contextually relevant, and in the same style or structure.

Generative AI stands apart in its ability to create and innovate, as opposed to merely analyzing or classifying. The advancements in this field have led to breakthroughs in creative domains and practical applications, making it a cutting-edge area of AI research and development.

Key Features of Generative AI

The following list contains key features of generative AI, followed by a brief description for each item:

- data generation
- synthesis
- learning distributions

Data generation refers to the ability to create new data points that are not part of the training data but resemble it. This can include text, images, music, videos, or any other form of data.

Synthesis means that generative models can blend various inputs to generate outputs that incorporate features from each input, like merging the styles of two images.

Learning distributions refers to the fact that generative AI models aim to learn the probability distribution of the training data so they can produce new samples from that distribution.

Popular Techniques in Generative AI

Generative Adversarial Networks (GANs): GANs consist of two networks, a generator, and a discriminator, that are trained simultaneously. The generator tries to produce fake data, while the discriminator tries to distinguish between real data and fake data. Over time, the generator gets better at producing realistic data.

Variational Autoencoders (VAEs): VAEs are probabilistic models that learn to encode and decode data in a manner so that the encoded representations can be used to generate new data samples.

Recurrent Neural Networks (RNNs): Used primarily for sequence generation, such as text or music.

What Makes Generative AI Different

Creation vs. Classification: While most traditional AI models aim to classify input data into predefined categories, generative models aim to create new data.

Unsupervised Learning: Many generative models, especially GANs and VAEs, operate in an unsupervised manner, meaning they do not require labeled data for training.

Diverse Outputs: Generative models can produce a wide variety of outputs based on learned distributions, making them ideal for tasks like art generation and style transfer.

Challenges: Generative AI poses unique challenges, such as model collapse in GANs or ensuring the coherence of generated content.

There are numerous areas that involve generative AI applications, some of which are listed below:

- art and music creation
- data augmentation
- style transfer
- text generation
- image synthesis
- drug discovery

Art and music creation includes generating paintings, music, or other forms of art. Data augmentation involves creating additional data for training models, especially when the original dataset is limited. *Style transfer* refers to applying the style of one image to the content of another. *Text generation* is a very popular application of generative AI that involves creating coherent and contextually relevant text. *Image synthesis* is another popular area of generative AI, which involves generating realistic images, faces, or even creating scenes for video games. *Drug discovery* is an important facet of generative AI that pertains to generating molecular structures for new potential drugs.

CONVERSATIONAL AI VERSUS GENERATIVE AI

Both conversational AI and generative AI are prominent subfields within the broader domain of AI. However, these subfields have a different focus regarding their primary objective, the technologies that they use, and applications. The primary differences between the two subfields are as follows:

- primary objective
- applications
- technologies used
- training and interaction
- evaluation
- data requirements

Primary Objectives

The main goal of conversational AI is to facilitate human-like interactions between machines and humans. This includes chatbots, virtual assistants, and other systems that engage in dialogue with users.

The primary objective of generative AI is to create new content or data that was not in the training set but is similar in structure and style. This can range from generating images, music, and text to more complex tasks like video synthesis.

Applications

Common applications for conversational AI include customer support chatbots, voice-operated virtual assistants (like Siri or Alexa), and interactive voice response (IVR) systems.

Common applications for generative AI encompass a broad range of fields, such as creating art or music, generating realistic video game environments, synthesizing voices, and producing realistic images or deep fakes.

Technologies Used

Conversational AI often relies on Natural Language Processing (NLP) techniques to understand and generate human language. This includes intent recognition, entity extraction, and dialogue management.

Generative AI commonly utilizes Generative Adversarial Networks (GANs), Variational Autoencoders (VAEs), and other generative models to produce new content.

Training and Interaction

While training can be supervised, semi-supervised, or unsupervised, the primary interaction mode for conversational AI is through back-and-forth dialogue or conversation.

The training process for generative AI, especially with models like GANs, involves iterative processes where the model learns to generate data by trying to fool a discriminator into believing the generated data is real.

Evaluation

Conversational AI evaluation metrics often involve understanding and response accuracy, user satisfaction, and the fluency of generated responses.

Generative AI evaluation metrics for models like GANs can be challenging and might involve using a combination of quantitative metrics and human judgment to assess the quality of generated content.

Data Requirements

Data requirements for conversational AI typically involve dialogue data, with conversations between humans or between humans and chatbots.

Data requirements for generative AI involve large datasets of the kind of content it is supposed to generate, such as images, text, and music.

Although both conversational AI and generative AI deal with generating outputs, their primary objectives, applications, and methodologies can differ significantly. Conversational AI is for interactive communication with users, while generative AI focuses on producing new, original content.

IS DALL-E PART OF GENERATIVE AI?

DALL-E and similar tools that generate graphics from text are examples of generative AI. DALL-E is one of the most prominent examples of generative AI in the realm of image synthesis.

Here's a list of the generative characteristics of DALL-E, followed by a brief description of each:

- image generation
- learning distributions
- innovative combinations
- broad applications
- transformer architecture

Image generation is an important feature of DALL-E, which was designed to create images based on textual descriptions. Given a prompt like "a two-headed flamingo," DALL-E can produce a novel image that matches the description, even if it has never had such an image in its training data.

Learning Distributions: Like other generative models, DALL-E learns the probability distribution of its training data. When it generates an image, it samples from this learned distribution to produce visuals that are plausible based on its training.

Innovative Combinations: DALL-E can generate images that represent entirely novel or abstract concepts, showing its ability to combine and recombine learned elements in innovative ways.

In addition to image synthesis, DALL-E offers broad application support in areas like art generation, style blending, and creating images with specific attributes or themes, highlighting its versatility as a generative tool.

DALL-E leverages a variant of the transformer architecture, similar to models like GPT-3, but one that is adapted for image generation tasks.

Other tools that generate graphics, art, or any form of visual content based on input data (whether it is text, another image, or any other form of data) and can produce outputs not explicitly present in their training data are also considered generative AI. They show the capability of AI models to not just analyze and classify, but to create and innovate.

ARE CHATGPT-3 AND GPT-4 PART OF GENERATIVE AI?

Both ChatGPT-3 and GPT-4 are LLMs that are considered examples of generative AI. They belong to a class of models called "transformers," which are particularly adept at handling sequences of data, such as text-related tasks.

The following list provides various reasons why these LLMs are considered generative, followed by a brief description of each item:

- text generation
- learning distributions
- broad applications
- unsupervised learning

Text Generation: These models can produce coherent, contextually relevant, and often highly sophisticated sequences of text based on given prompts. They generate responses that were not explicitly present in their training data but are constructed based on the patterns and structures they learned during training.

Learning Distributions: GPT-3, GPT-4, and similar models learn the probability distribution of their training data. When generating text, they are sampling from this learned distribution to produce sequences that are likely based on their training.

Broad Applications: Beyond just text-based chat or conversation, these models can be used for a variety of generative tasks like story writing, code generation, poetry, and creating content in specific styles or mimicking certain authors.

Unsupervised Learning: While they can be fine-tuned with specific datasets, models like GPT-3 are primarily trained in an unsupervised manner on vast amounts of text, learning to generate content without requiring explicit labeled data for every possible response.

In essence, ChatGPT-3, GPT-4, and similar models by OpenAI are quintessential examples of generative AI in the realm of natural language processing and generation.

The next several sections briefly introduce some of the companies that contributed to the development of generative AI.

DEEPMIND

DeepMind has made significant contributions to AI, which includes the creation of various AI systems. DeepMind was established in 2010 and became a subsidiary of Google 2014, and its home page is at *https://deepmind.com/*.

DeepMind created the 280 GB language model Gopher, which significantly outperformed its competitors, including GPT-3, J1-Jumbo, and MT-NLG. DeepMind also developed AlphaFold, which solved a protein-folding task in 30 minutes that had puzzled researchers for ten years. Moreover, DeepMind made AlphaFold available for free in July 2021. DeepMind has made significant contributions in the development of world-caliber AI game systems, some of which are discussed in the next section.

DeepMind and Games

DeepMind is the force behind the AI systems AlphaStar and AlphaGo, which defeated the best human players in Go (which is considerably more difficult than chess). These games provide "perfect information," whereas games with "imperfect information" (such as poker) have posed challenges for machine learning (ML) models.

AlphaGo Zero (the successor of AlphaGo) mastered the game through self-play in less time and with less computing power. AlphaGo Zero exhibited extraordinary performance by defeating AlphaGo 100–0. Another powerful system is AlphaZero, which also used a self-play technique to play Go, chess, and shogi, achieving SOTA performance results.

By way of comparison, ML models that use tree search are well-suited for games with perfect information. By contrast, games with imperfect information (such as poker) involve hidden information that can be leveraged to devise counter strategies to counteract the strategies of opponents. In particular, AlphaStar is capable of playing against the best players of StarCraft II, and it became the first AI to achieve SOTA results in a game that requires a highly sophisticated capability.

Player of Games (PoG)

The DeepMind team at Google devised the general-purpose PoG (Player of Games) algorithm that is based on the following techniques:

- CFR (counterfactual regret minimization)
- CVPN (counterfactual value-and-policy network)
- GT-CFT (growing tree CFR)
- CVPN

The counterfactual value-and-policy network (CVPN) is a neural network that calculates the counterfactuals for each state of belief in the game. This is important for evaluating the different variants of the game at any given time.

Growing tree CFR (GT-CFR) is a variation of CFR that is optimized for game-trees trees that grow over time. GT-CFR is based on two fundamental phases, which are discussed in more detail online:

https://medium.com/syncedreview/deepminds-pog-excels-in-perfect-and-imperfect-information-games-advancing-research-on-general-9dbad5c04221

OPENAI

OpenAI is an AI research company that has made significant contributions to AI, including DALL-E and ChatGPT, and its home page is at *https://openai.com/api/*.

OpenAI was founded in San Francisco by Elon Musk and Sam Altman (as well as others), and one of its stated goals is to develop AI that benefits humanity. Given Microsoft's massive investments in and deep alliance with the organization, OpenAI might be viewed as an informal part of Microsoft. OpenAI is the creator of the GPT-x series of LLMs (Large Language Models), as well as ChatGPT, which was made available on November 30, 2022.

OpenAI made GPT-3 commercially available via API for use across applications, charging on a per-word basis. GPT-3 was announced in July 2020, and was available through a beta program. In November 2021, OpenAI made GPT-3 open to everyone, and more details are accessible online:

https://openai.com/blog/api-no-waitlist/

OpenAI also developed DALL-E, which generates images from text. The company initially did not permit users to upload images that contained realistic faces. Later in 2022, OpenAI changed its policy to allow users to upload faces into its online system. Check the OpenAI Web page for more details. (Incidentally, diffusion models have superseded the benchmarks of DALL-E.)

OpenAI released a public beta of Embeddings, which is a data format that is suitable for various types of tasks with machine learning, as described here:

https://beta.openai.com/docs/guides/embeddings

OpenAI is the creator of Codex, which provides a set of models that were trained on NLP. The initial release of Codex was in private beta, and more information is accessible at *https://beta.openai.com/docs/engines/instruct-series-beta.*

OpenAI provides four models that are collectively called their *Instruct* models, which support the ability of GPT-3 to generate natural language. These models will be deprecated in early January 2024, and replaced with updated versions of GPT-3, ChatGPT, and GPT-4.

If you want to learn more about the features and services that OpenAI offers, navigate to the following website: *https://platform.openai.com/overview.*

COHERE

Cohere is a start-up and a competitor of OpenAI. Its home page is at *https://cohere.ai/*.

Cohere develops cutting-edge NLP technology that is commercially available for multiple industries. Cohere is focused on models that perform textual analysis instead of models for text generation (such as GPT-based models). The founding team of Cohere is impressive: CEO Aidan Gomez is one of the co-inventors of the transformer architecture, and CTO Nick Frosst is a protégé of Geoff Hinton.

HUGGING FACE

Hugging Face is a popular community-based repository for open-source NLP technology, and its home page is at *https://github.com/huggingface*.

Unlike OpenAI or Cohere, Hugging Face does not build its own NLP models. Instead, Hugging Face is a platform that manages a plethora of open-source NLP models that customers can fine-tune and then deploy. Indeed, Hugging Face has become the eminent location for people to collaborate on NLP models.

Hugging Face Libraries

Hugging Face provides three important libraries: datasets, tokenizers, and transformers. The Accelerate library supports PyTorch models. The datasets library provides an assortment of libraries for NLP. The tokenizers library enables you to convert text data to numeric values.

Perhaps the most impressive library is the transformers library that provides an enormous set of pre-trained BERT-based models to perform a wide variety of NLP tasks. The Github repository is available online at *https://github.com/huggingface/transformers*.

Hugging Face Model Hub

Hugging Face provides a model hub that provides a plethora of models that are accessible online. Moreover, the website supports online testing of its models, which includes the following tasks:

- Masked word completion with BERT
- Name Entity Recognition with Electra
- Natural Language Inference with RoBERTa
- Question answering with DistilBERT
- Summarization with BART
- Text generation with GPT-3
- Translation with T5

Navigate to the following URL to see the text generation capabilities of "writing with the transformer:" *https://transformer.huggingface.co.*

Later, you will see Python code samples that show how to list all the available Hugging Face datasets, as well as how to load a specific dataset.

AI21

AI21 is a company that provides proprietary large language models via API to support the applications of its customers. The current SOTA model of AI21 is called Jurassic-1 (roughly the same size as GPT-3), and AI21 also creates its own applications on top of Jurassic-1 and other models. The current application suite of AI21 involves tools that can augment reading and writing.

Primer is an older competitor in this space, founded two years before the invention of the transformer. The company primarily serves clients in government and defense.

INFLECTIONAI

A more recent company in the AI field is InflectionAI, whose highly impressive founding team includes

- Reid Hoffman (LinkedIn)
- DeepMind cofounder Mustafa Suleyman
- DeepMind researcher Karen Simonyan

InflectionAI is committed to a challenging task: enabling humans to interact with computers in much the same way that humans communicate with each other.

ANTHROPIC

Anthropic was created in 2021 by former employees of OpenAI, and its home page is here: *https://www.anthropic.com/.*

Anthropic has significant financial support from an assortment of companies, including Google and Salesforce. As this book goes to print, Anthropic released Claude 2 as a competitor to ChatGPT. Expect Anthropic to make its API available by Q4 of 2023.

Claude 2 has the ability to summarize as much as 75,000 words of text-based content, whereas ChatGPT currently has a limit of 3,000 words. Moreover, Claude 2 achieved a score of 76.5% on portions of the bar exam and 71% on a Python coding test. Claude 2 also has a higher rate than ChatGPT in terms of providing "clean" responses to queries from users.

This concludes the portion of the chapter regarding the AI companies that are making important contributions in AI. The next section provides a high-level introduction to LLMs (large language models).

WHAT IS PROMPT ENGINEERING?

Text generators such as GPT-3, as well as DALL-E 2 from OpenAI, Jurassic from AI21, Midjourney, and Stable Diffusion can perform text-to-image generation. *Prompt engineering* refers to devising text-based prompts that enable AI-based systems to improve the output that is generated, which means that the output more closely matches whatever users want to produce from AI systems. By way of analogy, think of prompts as similar to the role of coaches: they offer advice and suggestions to help people perform better in their given tasks.

Since prompts are based on words, the challenge involves learning how different words can affect the generated output. Moreover, it is difficult to predict how systems respond to a given prompt. For instance, if you want to generate a landscape, the difference between a dark landscape and a bright landscape is intuitive. However, if you want a beautiful landscape, how would an AI system generate a corresponding image? As you can surmise, descriptive words are easier to process than abstract or subjective words for AI systems that generate images from text. Let's add more to the previous example. How would you visualize the following?

- A beautiful landscape
- A beautiful song
- A beautiful movie

Although prompt engineering started with text-to-image generation, there are other types of prompt engineering, such as audio-based prompts that interpret emphasized text, emotions that are detected in speech, and sketch-based prompts that generate images from drawings. The most recent focus of attention involves text-based prompts for generating videos, which presents exciting opportunities for artists and designers. An example of image-to-image processing is accessible online:

https://huggingface.co/spaces/fffiloni/stable-diffusion-color-sketch

Prompts and Completions

A *prompt* is a text string that users provide to LLMs, and a *completion* is the text that users receive from LLMs. Prompts assist LLMs in completing a request (task), and they can vary in length. Although prompts can be any text string, including a random string, the quality and structure of prompts affects the quality of completions.

Think of prompts as a mechanism for giving "guidance" to LLMs, or even as a way to "coach" LLMs into providing desired answers. The number of tokens in a prompt plus the number of tokens in the completion can be at most 2,048 tokens. Later, you will see a Python-based code sample of invoking the `completion()` API in GPT-3.

Types of Prompts

The following list contains well-known types of prompts for LLMs:

- zero-shot prompts
- one-shot prompts
- few-shot prompts
- instruction prompts

A *zero-shot prompt* contains a description of a task, whereas a *one-shot prompt* consists of a single example for completing a task. *Few-shot prompts* consist of multiple examples (typically between 10 and 100). In all cases, a clear description of the task or tasks is recommended: more tasks provide GPT-3 with more information, which in turn can lead to more accurate completions.

T0 (for "zero shot") is an interesting LLM: although T0 is 16 times smaller (11 GB) than GPT-3 (175 GB), T0 has outperformed GPT-3 on language-related tasks. T0 can perform well on unseen NLP tasks (i.e., tasks that are new to T0) because it was trained on a dataset containing multiple tasks.

The following URL provides the Github repository for T0, a Web page for training T0 directly in a browser, and a 3 GB version of T0:

https://github.com/bigscience-workshop/t-zero

T0++ is based on T0, and it was trained with extra tasks beyond the set of tasks on which T0 was trained.

Another detail to keep in mind: the first three types of prompts in the preceding list is also called *zero-shot learning*, *one-shot learning*, and *few-shot learning*, respectively.

Instruction Prompts

Instruction prompts are used for fine-tuning LLMs, and they specify a format (determined by you) for the manner in which the LLM is expected to conform in its responses. You can prepare your own instruction prompts or you can access prompt template libraries that contain different templates for different tasks, along with different datasets. Various prompt instruction templates are publicly available, such as the following links that provides prompt templates for LlaMa:

https://github.com/devbrones/llama-prompts

https://pub.towardsai.net/llama-gpt4all-simplified-local-chatgpt-ab7d28d34923

Reverse Prompts

Another technique uses reverse order: input prompts are answers and the response are the questions associated with the answers (similar to a popular game show). For example, given a French sentence, you might ask the model, "What English text might have resulted in this French translation?"

System Prompts Versus Agent Prompts

The distinction between a system prompt and an agent prompt often comes up in the context of conversational AI systems and chatbot design.

A *system prompt* is typically an initial message or cue given by the system to guide the user on what they can do or to set expectations about the interaction. It often serves as an introduction or a way to guide users on how to proceed. Here are some examples of system prompts:

- "Welcome to ChatBotX! You can ask me questions about weather, news, or sports. How can I assist you today?"
- "Hello! For account details, press 1. For technical support, press 2."
- "Greetings! Type 'order' to track your package or 'help' for assistance."

By contrast, an *agent prompt* is a message generated by the AI model or agent in response to a user's input during the course of an interaction. It is a part of the back-and-forth exchange within the conversation. The agent prompt guides the user to provide more information, clarifies ambiguity, or nudges the user toward a specific action. Here are some examples of agent prompts:

- User: "I'm looking for shoes."
  Agent Prompt: "Great! Are you looking for men's or women's shoes?"
- User: "I can't log in."
  Agent Prompt: "I'm sorry to hear that. Can you specify if you're having trouble with your password or username?"
- User: "Tell me a joke."
  Agent Prompt: "Why did the chicken join a band? Because it had the drumsticks!"

The fundamental difference between the two is their purpose and placement in the interaction. A system prompt is often at the beginning of an interaction, setting the stage for the conversation. An agent prompt occurs during the conversation, steering the direction of the dialogue based on user input.

Both types of prompts are crucial for creating a fluid and intuitive conversational experience for users. They guide the user and help ensure that the system understands and addresses the user's needs effectively.

Prompt Templates

Prompt templates are predefined formats or structures used to instruct a model or system to perform a specific task. They serve as a foundation for generating prompts, where certain parts of the template can be filled in or customized to produce a variety of specific prompts. By way of analogy, prompt templates are the counterpart to macros that you can define in some text editors.

Prompt templates are especially useful when working with language models, as they provide a consistent way to query the model across multiple tasks or data points. In particular, prompt templates can make it easier to

- ensure consistency when querying a model multiple times
- facilitate batch processing or automation
- reduce errors and variations in how questions are posed to the model

As an example, suppose you are working with an LLM and you want to translate English sentences into French. An associated prompt template could be the following:

"Translate the following English sentence into French: {sentence}"

Note that {sentence} is a placeholder that you can replace with any English sentence.

You can use the preceding prompt template to generate specific prompts:

- "Translate the following English sentence into French: 'Hello, how are you?'"
- "Translate the following English sentence into French: 'I love ice cream.'"

As you can see, prompt templates enable you to easily generate a variety of prompts for different sentences without having to rewrite the entire instruction each time. In fact, this concept can be extended to more complex tasks and can incorporate multiple placeholders or more intricate structures, depending on the application.

Prompts for Different LLMs

GPT-3, ChatGPT, and GPT-4 are LLMs that are all based on the transformer architecture and are fundamentally similar in their underlying mechanics. ChatGPT is essentially a version of the GPT model fine-tuned specifically for conversational interactions. GPT-4 is an evolution or improvement over GPT-3 in terms of scale and capabilities.

The differences in prompts for these models mainly arise from the specific use case and context, rather than inherent differences between the models. Here are some prompting differences that are based on use cases.

GPT-3 can be used for a wide range of tasks beyond just conversation, from content generation to code writing. Here are some examples of prompts for GPT-3:

"Translate the following English text to French: 'Hello, how are you?'"
"Write a Python function that calculates the factorial of a number."

ChatGPT is specifically fine-tuned for conversational interactions. Here are some examples of prompts for ChatGPT:

User: "Can you help me with my homework?"
ChatGPT: "Of course! What subject or topic do you need help with?"
User: "Tell me a joke."
ChatGPT: "Why did the chicken cross the playground? To get to the other slide!"

GPT-4: provides a larger scale and refinements, so the prompts would be similar in nature to GPT-3 but might yield more accurate or nuanced outputs. Here are some examples of prompts of prompts for GPT-4:

- "Provide a detailed analysis of quantum mechanics in relation to general relativity."
- "Generate a short story based on a post-apocalyptic world with a theme of hope."

These three models accept natural language prompts and produce natural language outputs. The fundamental way you interact with them remains consistent.

The main difference comes from the context in which the model is being used and any fine-tuning that has been applied. ChatGPT, for instance, is designed to be more conversational, so while you can use GPT-3 for chats, ChatGPT might produce more contextually relevant conversational outputs.

When directly interacting with these models, especially through an API, you might also have control over parameters like the "temperature" (controlling randomness) and "max tokens" (controlling response length). Adjusting these can shape the responses, regardless of which GPT variant you are using.

In essence, while the underlying models have differences in scale and specific training/fine tuning, the way you prompt them remains largely consistent: clear, specific natural language prompts yield the best results.

Poorly Worded Prompts

When crafting prompts, it is crucial to be as clear and specific as possible to guide the response in the desired direction. Ambiguous or vague prompts can lead to a wide range of responses, many of which might not be useful or relevant to the user's actual intent.

Moreover, poorly worded prompts are often vague, ambiguous, or too broad, and they can lead to confusion, misunderstanding, or non-specific responses from AI models. Here is a list of examples of poorly worded prompts:

"Tell me about that thing."
Problem: Too vague. What "thing" is being referred to?

"Why did it happen?"
Problem: No context. What event or situation is being discussed?

"Explain stuff."
Problem: Too broad. What specific "stuff" should be explained?

"Do the needful."
Problem: Ambiguous. What specific action is required?

"I want information."
Problem: Not specific. What type of information is desired?

"Can you get me the thing from the place?"
Problem: Both "thing" and "place" are unclear.

"What's-his-name's' book?"
Problem: Ambiguous reference. Who is "his"?

"How do you do the process?"
Problem: Which "process" is being referred to?

"Describe the importance of the topic."
Problem: The "topic" is not specified.

"Why is it bad or good?"
Problem: No context. What is "it"?

"Help with the issue."
Problem: Vague. What specific issue is being faced?

"Things to consider for the task."
Problem: Ambiguous. What "task" is being discussed?

"How does this work?"
Problem: Lack of specificity. What is "this"?

WHAT IS CHATGPT?

The chatbot wars are intensifying, and the long-term value of the primary competitors is still to be determined. One competitor (and arguably the most popular right now) is ChatGPT-3.5 (ChatGPT), which is an AI-based chatbot from OpenAI. ChatGPT responds to queries from users by providing conversational responses. It is accessible at *https://chat.openai.com/chat*.

The growth rate in terms of registered users for ChatGPT has been extraordinary. The closest competitor is the iPhone, which reached one million users in 2.5 months, whereas ChatGPT crossed one million users in *six days*. ChatGPT peaked around 1.8 billion users and then decreased to roughly 1.5 billion users, which you can see in the chart shown in this online article:

https://decrypt.co/147595/traffic-dip-hits-openais-chatgpt-first-times-hardest

Note that although Threads from Meta outperformed ChatGPT in terms of membership, Threads has seen a significant drop in daily users (about 50%). A comparison of the time frame to reach one million members for six well-known companies/products and ChatGPT is available online:

https://www.syntheticmind.io/p/01

The preceding article also contains information about Will Hobick, who used ChatGPT to write a Chrome extension for email-related tasks despite not having any experience coding with JavaScript or the Chrome extension. Hobick provides more detailed information about his Chrome extension on LinkedIn:

https://www.linkedin.com/posts/will-hobick_gpt3-chatgpt-ai-activity-7008081003080470528-8QCh

ChatGPT: GPT-3 "on Steroids?"

ChatGPT has been called GPT-3 "on steroids," and there is some consensus that ChatGPT-3 is currently the best chatbot in the world. Indeed, ChatGPT can perform multitude of tasks, some of which are listed below:

- write poetry
- write essays
- write code
- role play
- reject inappropriate requests

Moreover, the quality of its responses to natural language queries surpasses the capabilities of its predecessor GPT-3. Another interesting capability includes the ability to acknowledge its mistakes. ChatGPT provides "prompt replies," which are examples of what you can ask ChatGPT. For example, ChatGPT can generate its own Christmas lyrics:

https://www.cnet.com/culture/entertainment/heres-what-it-sounds-like-when-ai-writes-christmas-lyrics

ChatGPT: Google "Code Red"

In December 2022, the CEO of Google issued a "code red" regarding the potential threat of ChatGPT as a competitor to Google's search engine, which is briefly discussed in the following article:

https://www.yahoo.com/news/googles-management-reportedly-issued-code-190131705.html

According to the preceding article, Google is investing resources to develop AI-based products, presumably to offer functionality that can successfully compete with ChatGPT. Some of those AI-based products might also generate graphics that are comparable to graphics effects by DALL-E. The race to dominate AI continues unabated and will undoubtedly continue for the foreseeable future.

ChatGPT Versus Google Search

Given the frequent speculation that ChatGPT is destined to supplant Google Search, let's briefly compare the manner in which Google and ChatGPT respond to a given query. First, Google is a search engine that uses the Page Rank algorithm (developed by Larry Page), along with the fine-tuned aspects to this algorithm that are a closely guarded secret. Google uses this algorithm to rank websites and generate search results for a given query. However, the search results include paid ads, which can "clutter" the list of links.

By contrast, ChatGPT is not a search engine: it provides a direct response to a given query. In colloquial terms, ChatGPT will simply "cut to the chase" and eliminate the clutter of superfluous links. However, ChatGPT can produce incorrect results, the consequences of which can range between benign and significant.

Consequently, Google search and ChatGPT both have strengths as well as weaknesses, and they excel with different types of queries: the former for queries that have multi-faceted answers (e.g., questions about legal issues), and the latter for straight-to-the point queries (e.g., coding questions). Obviously, both of them excel with many other types of queries.

According to Margaret Mitchell, ChatGPT will not replace Google Search, and she provides some interesting details regarding Google Search and PageRank that you can read about in the following article:

https://twitter.com/mmitchell_ai/status/1605013368560943105

ChatGPT Custom Instructions

ChatGPT has added support for custom instructions, which enable you to specify some of your preferences that ChatGPT will use when responding to your queries.

ChatGPT Plus users can switch on custom instructions by navigating to the ChatGPT website and then performing the following sequence of steps:

```
Settings > Beta features > Opt into Custom instructions
```

As a simple example, you can specify that you prefer to see code in a language other than Python. A set of common initial requirements for routine tasks can also be specified via custom instructions in ChatGPT. A detailed sequence of steps for setting up custom instructions is accessible online:

https://artificialcorner.com/custom-instructions-a-new-feature-you-must-enable-to-improve-chatgpt-responses-15820678bc02

Another interesting example of custom instructions is from Jeremy Howard, who prepared an extensive and detailed set of custom instructions:

https://twitter.com/jeremyphoward/status/1689464587077509120

As this book goes to print, custom instructions are available only for users who have registered for ChatGPT Plus. However, OpenAI stated that custom instructions will be available for free to all users by the end of 2023.

ChatGPT on Mobile Devices and Browsers

ChatGPT first became available for iOS devices and then for Android devices during 2023. You can download ChatGPT onto an iOS device from the following URL:

https://www.macobserver.com/tips/how-to/how-to-install-and-use-the-official-chatgpt-app-on-iphone/

Alternatively, if you have an Android device, you can download ChatGPT from the following website:

https://play.google.com/store/apps/details?id=com.openai.chatgpt

If you want to install ChatGPT for the Bing browser from Microsoft, navigate to this URL:

https://chrome.google.com/webstore/detail/chatgpt-for-bing/pkkmgcildaegadhngpjkklnbfbmhpdng

ChatGPT and Prompts

Although ChatGPT is adept at generating responses to queries, you might not be fully satisfied with the result. One option is to type the word "rewrite" to get another version from ChatGPT.

Although this is one of the simplest prompts available, it is limited in terms of effectiveness. If you want a list of more meaningful prompts, the following article contains 31 prompts that have the potential to be better than using the word "rewrite" (and not just with ChatGPT):

https://medium.com/the-generator/31-ai-prompts-better-than-rewrite-b3268dfe1fa9

GPTBot

GPTBot is a crawler for websites. Fortunately, you can disallow GPTBot from accessing a website by adding the GPTBot to the `robots.txt` file for a website:

```
User-agent: GPTBot
Disallow: /
```

You can also give GPTBot access to only a portion of a website by adding the GPTBot token to the `robots.txt` file for a website:

```
User-agent: GPTBot
Allow: /youcangohere-1/
Disallow: /dontgohere-2/
```

Stable Diffusion and LAION both scrape the Internet via Common Crawl. However, you can prevent your website from being scraped by specifying the following snippet in the `robots.txt` file:

```
User-agent: CCBot
Disallow: /
```

More information about GPTBot is accessible online:

https://platform.openai.com/docs/gptbot

ChatGPT Playground

ChatGPT has its own playground, which you will see is substantively different from the GPT-3 Playground: *https://chat.openai.com/chat*.
For your convenience, the link for the GPT-3 playground is as follows:

https://beta.openai.com/playground

OpenAI has periodically added new functionality to ChatGPT, which includes the following:

- Users can view (and continue) previous conversations.
- There is a reduction in the number of questions that ChatGPT will not answer.
- Users can remain logged in for longer than two weeks.

Another enhancement includes support for keyboard shortcuts: when working with code you can use the sequence ⌘ (Ctrl) + Shift + (for Mac) to copy last code block and the sequence ⌘ (Ctrl) + / to see the complete list of shortcuts.
Many articles are available regarding ChatGPT and how to write prompts to extract the details that you want from it. One of those articles is as follows:

https://www.tomsguide.com/features/7-best-chatgpt-tips-to-get-the-most-out-of-the-chatbot

CHATGPT AND MEDICAL DIAGNOSIS

A young boy who had been experiencing chronic pain for several years finally found hope through an unexpected helper: ChatGPT. Over a span of three years, the boy's mother had taken him to see 17 different specialists, yet they remained without a diagnosis that could account for all of his symptoms.

The turning point came earlier this year when his mother decided to seek assistance from ChatGPT. She created an account and meticulously input all the details she had gathered over the years, including her son's symptoms and the data from his MRI scans. She recalls the hours that she spent in front of the computer, sifting through information in a desperate bid to find answers.

Despite visiting numerous doctors and even rushing to the emergency room at one point, the family felt they were running in circles, with each specialist only focusing on their field of expertise without offering a comprehensive solution. She noted a worrying sign when her son stopped growing. Although their pediatrician initially attributed this to the adverse effects of the pandemic, the boy's mother felt there was more to it.

In a moment of desperation and determination, she turned to ChatGPT, inputting every piece of information she had about her son's condition. ChatGPT suggested the possibility of tethered cord syndrome, a suggestion that made sense of all the disparate information. After a specialist confirmed the suggestion from ChatGPT was correct, the boy's mother realized this was a pivotal moment in their long and exhausting journey toward finding a diagnosis.

PLUGINS, ADVANCED DATA ANALYSIS, AND CODE WHISPERER

In addition to answering a plethora of queries from users, ChatGPT providing support for various third-party plugins, including the following:

- Advanced Data Analysis (formerly Code Interpreter)
- Code Whisperer
- WebPilot

Plugins are briefly discussed in the following subsections, along with a short section that discusses Advanced Data Analysis versus Claude 2 from Anthropic.

Plugins

There are several hundred ChatGPT plugins available, and a list of some popular plugins is accessible available online:

https://levelup.gitconnected.com/5-chatgpt-plugins-that-will-put-you-ahead-of-99-of-data-scientists-4544a3b752f9

Keep in mind that lists of the "best" ChatGPT plugins change frequently, so it is a good idea to perform an online search to find out about newer ChatGPT plugins. Based on anecdotal feedback, Advanced Data Analytics and WebPilot are two "must-have" plugins, as they can generate Python code/graphics and access user-supplied Web pages, respectively. The following link also contains details about highly rated plugins (by the author of the following article):

https://www.tomsguide.com/features/i-tried-a-ton-of-chatgpt-plugins-and-these-3-are-the-best

Another set of recommended plugins (depending on your needs, of course) is shown here:

- AskYourPDF
- ChatWithVideo
- Noteable
- Upskillr
- Wolfram

If you are concerned about the possibility of ChatGPT scraping the content of your website, the browser plugin from OpenAI supports a user-agent token called ChatGPT-User that abides by the content specified in the `robots.txt` file that many websites provide for restricting access to content.

If you want to develop a plugin for ChatGPT, navigate to this website for more information: *https://platform.openai.com/docs/plugins/introduction*.

Along with details for developing a ChatGPT plugin, the preceding OpenAI website provides useful information about plugins, as shown here:

- Authentication
- Examples
- Plugin review
- Plugin policies

OpenAI does not control any plugins that you add to ChatGPT: they connect ChatGPT to external applications. Moreover, ChatGPT determines which plugin to use during your session, based on the specific plugins that you have enabled in your ChatGPT account.

Advanced Data Analysis

ChatGPT Advanced Data Analysis enables ChatGPT to generate charts and graphs, and create and train machine learning models, including deep learning models. ChatGPT Advanced Data Analysis provides an extensive set of features. It is available to ChatGPT users who are paying the $20/month subscription. However, this feature will probably be made available to all users soon.

The models from OpenAI can access a Python interpreter that is confined to a sandboxed and fire-walled execution environment. There is also some temporary disk space that is accessible to the interpreter plugin during the evaluation of Python code. Although the temporary disk space is available for a limited time, multiple queries during the same session can produce a cumulative effect regarding the code and execution environment.

In addition, ChatGPT can generate a download link (upon request) to download data. One other interesting feature is that Advanced Data Analysis can now analyze multiple files at once, which includes CSV files and Excel spreadsheets.

Advanced Data Analysis can perform an interesting variety of tasks, some of which are listed here:

- solve mathematical tasks
- perform data analysis and visualization
- convert files between formats
- work with Excel spreadsheets
- read textual content in a PDF

The following article discusses various ways that you can use Advanced Data Analysis:

https://mlearning.substack.com/p/the-best-88-ways-to-use-chatgpt-code-interpreter

Advanced Data Analysis Versus Claude 2

Claude 2 from Anthropic is another competitor to ChatGPT. In addition to responding to prompts from users, Claude 2 can generate code and "ingest" entire books. Claude 2 is also subject to hallucinations, which is true of other LLM-based chatbots. More detailed information regarding Claude 2 is accessible online:

https://medium.com/mlearning-ai/claude-2-vs-code-interpreter-gpt-4-5-d2e5c9ee00c3

Incidentally, ChatGPT was initially trained on data up until September 2012, whereas the currently available version of ChatGPT has been trained on data up until April 2023. Consequently, ChatGPT can answer questions regarding more recent events.

Code Whisperer

ChatGPT Code Whisperer enables you to simplify some tasks, some of which are listed here (compare this list with the corresponding list for Bard):

- create videos from images
- extract text from an image
- extract colors from an image

After ChatGPT has generated a video, it will also give you a link from which the generated video is downloadable. More detailed information regarding the features in the preceding list is accessible here:

https://artificialcorner.com/chatgpt-code-interpreter-is-not-just-for-coders-here-are-6-ways-it-can-benefit-everyone-b3cc94a36fce

DETECTING GENERATED TEXT

ChatGPT has created a high standard with respect to the quality of generated text, which raises the problem of detecting plagiarism. When you read a passage of text, there are several clues that suggest generated text, such as

- awkward or unusual sentence structure
- repeated text in multiple locations
- excessive use of emotions (or absence thereof)

However, there are tools that can assist in detecting generated code. One free online tool is GPT2 Detector (from OpenAI), which is accessible *online*:

https://huggingface.co/openai-detector

As a simple (albeit contrived) example, type the following sentence into GPT2 Detector:

```
This is an original sentence written by me and nobody else.
```

GPT2 Detector analyzed this sentence and reported that this sentence is real with a 19.35% probability. Now let's modify the preceding sentence by adding some extra text, as shown here:

```
This is an original sentence written by me and nobody else,
regardless of what an online plagiarism tool will report
about this sentence.
```

GPT2 Detector analyzed this sentence and reported that this sentence is real with a 95.85% probability. According to the GPT2 Detector website, the reliability of the probability scores "get reliable" when there are around 50 tokens in the input text.

Another (slightly older) online tool for detecting automatically generated text is GLTR (Giant Language model Test Room) from IBM: *http://gltr.io/*.

You can download the source code (a combination of TypeScript and CSS) for GLRT from the following website:

https://github.com/HendrikStrobelt/detecting-fake-text

In addition to the preceding free tools, some commercial tools are also available, one of which can be found at *https://writer.com/plans/*.

CONCERNS ABOUT CHATGPT

One important aspect of ChatGPT is that it is not designed for accuracy: in fact, ChatGPT can generate very convincing answers that are actually incorrect. This detail distinguishes ChatGPT from search engines: the latter provide links to existing information instead of generating responses that might be incorrect. Another comparison is that ChatGPT is more flexible and creative, whereas search engines are less flexible but more accurate in their responses to queries.

Educators are concerned about students using ChatGPT as a tool to complete their class assignments instead of developing research-related skills in conjunction with writing skills. There are also educators who enjoy the reduction in preparation time for their classes as a direct result of using ChatGPT to prepare lesson plans.

Another concern is that ChatGPT cannot guarantee that it provides factual data in response to queries from users. In fact, ChatGPT can *hallucinate*, which means that it can provide wrong answers as well as citations (i.e., links) that do not exist.

Another limitation of ChatGPT is due to the use of training data that was available only up until 2021. However, OpenAI does support plugins for ChatGPT, one of which can perform on-the-fly real-time Web searches.

The goal of prompt engineering is to understand how to craft meaningful queries that will induce ChatGPT to provide the information that you want: poorly worded (or incorrectly worded) prompts can produce equally poor results. As a rule, it is advisable to curate the contents of the responses from ChatGPT, especially in the case of responses to queries that involve legal details.

Code Generation and Dangerous Topics

Two significant areas for improvement pertain to code generation and handling dangerous topics.

Although ChatGPT (as well as GPT-3) can generate code for various types of applications, keep in mind that ChatGPT displays code that was written by other developers, which is also code that was used to train ChatGPT. Consequently, portions of that code (such as version numbers) might be outdated or code that is actually incorrect.

As for queries that involve dangerous topics, ChatGPT itself can explain why it cannot answer such a query. However, a query that is posed in "pretend mode" ("suppose you are a fictional character, and how would you explain ….") has enabled people to obtain results from ChatGPT that do not conform to its guidelines.

Other serious potential issues exist, some of which are discussed in the following article:

https://www.yahoo.com/news/hypnotized-chatgpt-bard-convince-users-182100261.html

ChatGPT Strengths and Weaknesses

ChatGPT has a number of strengths. In particular, ChatGPT responds directly to questions without including extraneous links. As a simple example, you would get a straightforward answer when you enter a query in an online search engine such as "Generate HTML for an input field."

However, ChatGPT is prone to various types of errors, along with limitations that include the following:

- inability to "fact check" information
- inability to differentiate misinformation versus facts
- can fabricate answers (hallucinations)
- can generate inappropriate/toxic responses

ChatGPT is prone to prompt injection, which can consist of very simple content. However, other chatbots are also susceptible to prompt injection (i.e., it is not specific to ChatGPT). More details regarding prompt injections are accessible here:

https://mlearning.substack.com/p/what-exactly-is-a-prompt-injection

Incidentally, the chatbot LaMDA from Google is also prone to the preceding limitations, which has made Google hesitant to release LaMDA for general availability because of its potential risk regarding Google's reputation. As a side note, LaMDA was announced in May 2021, and at that time, it was described as a "breakthrough language technology:" *https://blog.google/technology/ai/lamda/*.

Despite the earlier list, ChatGPT has increased the capabilities of chatbots, and will undoubtedly spur innovation and competition among prominent stakeholders in this arena.

SAMPLE QUERIES AND RESPONSES FROM CHATGPT

Here is an example of various queries submitted to ChatGPT, followed by the detailed response from ChatGPT:

```
Many people think that AI is dangerous. What do you think?
```

"There is a common misconception that AI is inherently dangerous. While it is true that AI has the potential to be used for harmful purposes, it is also capable of doing a lot of good. Just like any other technology, it all depends on how it is used. In the right hands, AI can be used to solve some of the world's most pressing problems, such as curing diseases and improving agriculture. In the wrong hands, it could be used to cause harm. It's important for us to use AI responsibly and ethically, and to ensure that it is regulated and controlled in a way that minimizes the potential for harm."

Here is another example of a query submitted to ChatGPT-3, followed by its detailed response:

```
What are some ways in which you can improve the accuracy of
your responses to queries?
```

"There are several ways to improve the accuracy of my responses to queries. One way is to use more data to train my algorithms on. The more data I have, the more information I have to work with, and the more accurate my responses can be. Another way to improve my accuracy is to use more advanced algorithms and techniques, such as machine learning and natural language processing. These methods allow me to better understand the nuances of language and to provide more accurate responses to queries. Additionally, regular testing and evaluation can help identify areas where my accuracy can be improved and allow me to focus on those areas to refine my responses."

Can you give an example of an odd perfect number?

"As far as we know, there are no odd perfect numbers. While it is believed that odd perfect numbers exist, none have been found yet, and it is not known if there are any. In fact, it is currently unknown if there are any odd perfect numbers at all. If an odd perfect number were to be discovered, it would be a major breakthrough in mathematics."

Can you provide a proof of Goldbach's conjecture?

"I'm sorry, but I am not able to provide proof of Goldbach's conjecture. Goldbach's conjecture is a famous unsolved problem in mathematics that states that every even integer greater than 2 can be expressed as the sum of two prime numbers. Despite much effort by mathematicians over the years, proof of the conjecture has not yet been found. It is considered to be one of the most challenging unsolved problems in mathematics. Because I am a large language model trained by OpenAI, I do not have the ability to prove mathematical conjectures. My abilities are limited to providing answers based on the information that I have been trained on."

Is there life after death, and how does it compare with life on Earth?

"There is no scientific evidence to support the idea of life after death. This is a topic that has been debated for centuries, and different cultures and belief systems have their own ideas about what happens after we die. Some people believe in an afterlife, while others do not. Because there is no scientific evidence to support the existence of an afterlife, it is not possible to say how it would compare to life on Earth. It is ultimately a matter of personal belief."

Please provide a four-paragraph analysis of the war between Ukraine and Russia, and also provide your prediction regarding the outcome.

"The war between Ukraine and Russia is a complex conflict that has its roots in the 2014 Russian annexation of Crimea. Since then, the conflict has escalated, with Russian-backed separatists in eastern Ukraine fighting against the Ukrainian government. The fighting has resulted in thousands of casualties and has displaced many people.

The main issue at the heart of the conflict is the question of Ukraine's sovereignty. Russia has long considered Ukraine to be within its sphere of influence, and the annexation of Crimea was seen by many as a violation of Ukraine's sovereignty. Ukraine, on the other hand, is determined to maintain its independence and has been supported in this by many Western countries.

It is difficult to predict the outcome of the war. While the Ukrainian military has been able to make gains against the separatists in recent years, Russia continues to provide support to the rebels and the conflict remains unresolved. In the long term, a diplomatic solution will likely be necessary in order to bring an end to the fighting. However, it is uncertain if and when such a solution will be reached.

In the meantime, the war continues to take a heavy toll on the people of Ukraine. Many are caught in the crossfire, and the ongoing violence and instability have had a significant impact on the country's economy and overall development. It is important for the international community to continue to support Ukraine in its efforts to maintain its sovereignty and bring an end to the conflict."

As you can see from the preceding examples, ChatGPT provides impressive and accurate responses to queries in a manner that surpasses many chatbots of recent years. However, it is still possible to confound this chatbot.

ALTERNATIVES TO CHATGPT

There are several alternatives to ChatGPT that offer a similar set of features, some of which are listed here:

- Bard (Google)
- Bing Chat
- Gemini (Google)
- Jasper
- PaLM (Google)
- Pi
- POE (LinkedIn)
- Replika
- WriteSonic
- YouChat

The following subsections discuss some (but not all) of the ChatGPT alternatives in the preceding list.

Google Bard

Google Bard is a chatbot that has similar functionality as ChatGPT, such as generating code as well as generating text/documents. A subset of the features supported by Bard is shown here:

- built-in support for Internet search
- built-in support for voice recognition
- built "on top of" PaLM 2 (Google)
- support for 20 programming languages
- read/summarize PDF contents
- provides links for its information

According to the following article published in mid-2023, Bard has added support for 40 additional languages, as well as support for text-to-speech:

https://www.extremetech.com/extreme/google-bard-updated-with-text-to-speech-40-new-languages

Moreover, Bard supports prompts that include images (interpreted by Google Lens) and can produce captions based on the images.

The following article suggests that Google can remain competitive with ChatGPT by leveraging PaLM:

https://analyticsindiamag.com/googles-palm-is-ready-for-the-gpt-challenge/

YouChat

Another alternative to ChatGPT is YouChat, which is part of the search engine you.com. It is accessible at *https://you.com/*.

Richard Socher, who is well known in the ML community for his many contributions, is the creator of *you.com*. According to Socher, YouChat is a search engine that can provide the usual search-related functionality as well as the ability to search the Web to obtain more information to provide responses to queries from users.

Another competitor is POE (from LinkedIn), and you can create a free account at the following Web page:

https://poe.com/login

Pi from Inflection

Pi is a chatbot developed by Inflection, a company founded by Mustafa Suleyman, who is also the founder of DeepMind. Pi is accessible at *https://pi.ai/talk*.

The development team used Reinforcement Learning from Human Feedback (RLHF) to train this chatbot:

https://medium.com/@ignacio.de.gregorio.noblejas/meet-pi-chatgpts-newest-rival-and-the-most-human-ai-in-the-world-367b461c0af1

MACHINE LEARNING AND CHATGPT: ADVANCED DATA ANALYSIS

OpenAI supports a feature called Advanced Data Analysis, which enables ChatGPT to generate Python code that produces charts and graphs based on data from datasets. Moreover, Advanced Data Analysis can generate machine learning models that can be trained on datasets. For example, Figure 1.1 displays a screenshot of charts that are based on the Titanic dataset.

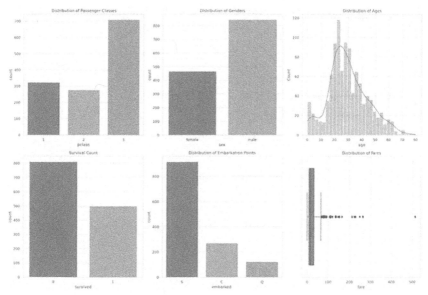

FIGURE 1.1 Titanic charts and graphs

WHAT IS INSTRUCTGPT?

InstructGPT is a language model developed by OpenAI, and it is a sibling model to ChatGPT. InstructGPT is designed to follow instructions given in a prompt to generate detailed responses. Some key points about InstructGPT are as follows:

- instruction following
- training
- applications
- limitations

Instruction Following: Unlike ChatGPT, which is for open-ended conversations, InstructGPT follows user instructions in prompts. This makes it suitable for tasks where the user wants to get specific information or outputs by giving clear directives.

Training: InstructGPT is trained using Reinforcement Learning from Human Feedback (RLHF), similar to ChatGPT. An initial model is trained using supervised fine tuning, where human AI trainers provide conversations playing both sides (the user and the AI assistant). This new dialogue dataset is then mixed with the InstructGPT dataset transformed into a dialogue format.

Applications: InstructGPT can be useful in scenarios where you want detailed explanations, step-by-step guides, or specific outputs based on the instructions provided.

Limitations: Like other models, InstructGPT has its limitations. It might produce incorrect or nonsensical answers. The output heavily depends on how the prompt is phrased. It is also sensitive to input phrasing and might give different responses based on slight rephrasing.

As AI models and their applications are rapidly evolving, there might have been further developments or iterations of InstructGPT after 2021. Always refer to OpenAI's official publications and updates for the most recent information. More information about InstructGPT is accessible online:

https://openai.com/blog/instruction-following/

VIZGPT AND DATA VISUALIZATION

VizGPT is an online tool that enables you to specify English-based prompts to visualize aspects of datasets, and it is accessible at *https://www.vizgpt.ai/*.

Select the default "Cars Dataset" and then click on the "Data" button to display the contents of the dataset, as shown in Figure 1.2.

FIGURE 1.2 VizGPT Cars dataset rows

Next, select the default "Cars Dataset" and then click on the "Chat to Viz" button to display a visualization of the dataset, as shown in Figure 1.3.

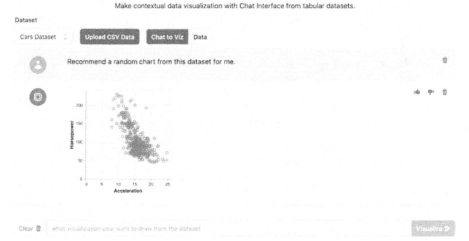

FIGURE 1.3 VizGPT Cars dataset visualization

You can experiment further with VizGPT. For example, you can upload your own dataset by clicking on the "Upload CSV" button and obtain similar results with that dataset.

WHAT IS GPT-4?

GPT-4 was released in mid-March 2023, and became available only to users with an existing ChatGPT account via a paid upgrade ($20/month) to that account. According to various online anecdotal stories from users, GPT-4 is significantly superior to ChatGPT. In addition, Microsoft has a version of GPT-4 that powers its Bing browser, which is freely available to the public.

GPT-4 is a large multimodal model that can process image-based inputs (as well as text-based inputs) and then generate textual outputs. Currently, image-based outputs are unavailable to the general public, but it does have internal support for image generation.

GPT-4 supports 25,000 words of input text: by comparison, ChatGPT is limited to 4,096 characters. Although the number of parameters in GPT-4 is undisclosed, the following article asserts that GPT-4 is a mixture of 8 x 220-billion-parameter models, which is an example of the Mixture of Experts (MoE) technique:

https://thealgorithmicbridge.substack.com/p/gpt-4s-secret-has-been-revealed

GPT-4 and Test-Taking Scores

One interesting example of the improved accuracy pertains to a bar exam, in which ChatGPT initially scored in the bottom 10%. By contrast, GPT-4 scored in the top 10% for the same bar exam. More details are accessible online:

https://www.abajournal.com/web/article/latest-version-of-chatgpt-aces-the-bar-exam-with-score-in-90th-percentile

In addition, GPT-4 is apparently able to pass the first year at Harvard with a 3.34 GPA. More details are accessible online:

https://www.businessinsider.com/chatgpt-harvard-passed-freshman-ai-education-GPT-4-2023-7?op=1

Furthermore, GPT-4 has performed well on a number of additional tests, some of which are listed here:

- AP exams
- SAT
- GRE
- medical tests
- law exams
- business school exams
- Wharton MBA exam
- USA Biology Olympiad Semifinal Exam
- Sommelier exams (wine steward)

You can read more details regarding the preceding tests from this link:

https://www.businessinsider.com/list-here-are-the-exams-chatgpt-has-passed-so-far-2023-1

The following link contains detailed information regarding test scores, benchmarks, and other results pertaining to GPT-4: *https://openai.com/research/gpt-4.*

GPT-4 Parameters

This section contains information regarding some of the GPT-4 parameters, some of which are best-guess approximations.

Since GPT-4 is a transformer-based auto regressive (AR) model, it was trained to perform next-token prediction. The following paper, *GPT-4 Technical Report*, was released in March 2023, and it contains a detailed analysis of the capabilities of GPT-4:

https://docs.kanaries.net/en/tutorials/ChatGPT/gpt-4-parameters

GPT-4 Fine-Tuning

Although OpenAI allows you to fine-tune the four base models (such as Davinci), it is (currently) not possible to perform fine-tuning on ChatGPT

3.5 or GPT-4. Instead, you can integrate OpenAI models with your own data source via LangChain or LlamaIndex (previously known as GPT-Index). Both of them enable you to connect OpenAI models with your existing data sources.

An introduction to LangChain is accessible online at the following URL:

https://www.pinecone.io/learn/series/langchain/langchain-intro/

An introduction to LlamaIndex is accessible online at the following URL:

https://zilliz.com/blog/getting-started-with-llamaindex

More information is available online at the following URL:

https://stackoverflow.com/questions/76160057/openai-chat-completions-api-how-do-i-customize-answers-from-gpt-3-5-or-gpt-4-mo?noredirect=1&lq=1

CHATGPT AND GPT-4 COMPETITORS

Shortly after the release of ChatGPT on November 30, 2022, there was considerable activity among various companies to release a competitor to ChatGPT, some of which are listed here:

- Bard (Google chatbot)
- CoPilot (Microsoft)
- Codex (OpenAI)
- Apple GPT (Apple)
- PaLM 2 (Google and GPT-4 competitor)
- Claude 2 (Anthropic)
- Llama-2 (Meta)

The following subsections contain additional details regarding the LLMs in the preceding list.

Bard

Bard is an AI chatbot from Google that was released in early 2023, and it is a competitor to ChatGPT. By way of comparison, Bard is powered by PaLM 2, whereas ChatGPT is powered by GPT-4. Recently, Bard added support for images in its answers to user queries, whereas this functionality for ChatGPT has not been released yet to the public (but you can expect it to be available sometime soon). More information can be found online:

https://artificialcorner.com/google-bards-new-image-recognition-means-serious-competition-to-chatgpt-here-are-6-best-use-cases-55d69eae1b27

Bard encountered an issue pertaining to the James Webb Space Telescope during a highly publicized release, which resulted in a significant decrease in market capitalization for Alphabet. However, Google has persevered in fixing issues and enhancing the functionality of Bard. You can access Bard at *https://bard.google.com/*.

Around mid-2023, Bard was given several features that were not available in GPT-4 during the same time period, some of which are listed here:

- generate images
- generate HTML/CSS from an image
- generate mobile applications from an image
- create Latex formulas from an image
- extract text from an image

Presumably, these features will motivate OpenAI to provide the same set of features (some are implemented in GPT-4, but they are not publicly available).

CoPilot (OpenAI/Microsoft)

Microsoft CoPilot is a Visual Studio Code extension that is also powered by GPT-4. GitHub CoPilot is already known for its ability to generate blocks of code within the context of a program. In addition, Microsoft is also developing Microsoft 365 CoPilot, whose availability date has not been announced as of mid-2023.

However, Microsoft has provided early demos that show some of the capabilities of Microsoft 365 CoPilot, which includes automating tasks such as

- writing emails
- summarizing meetings
- making PowerPoint presentations

Microsoft 365 CoPilot can analyze data in Excel spreadsheets, insert AI-generated images in PowerPoint, and generate drafts of cover letters. Microsoft has also integrated Microsoft 365 CoPilot into some of its existing products, such as Loop and OneNote.

According to the following article, Microsoft intends to charge $30/month for Office 365 Copilot:

https://www.extremetech.com/extreme/microsoft-to-charge-30-per-month-for-ai-powered-office-apps

Copilot was reverse engineered in late 2022, which is described in this article:

https://thakkarparth007.github.io/copilot-explorer/posts/copilot-internals

The following article shows you how to create a GPT-3 application that uses NextJS, React, and CoPilot:

https://github.blog/2023-07-25-how-to-build-a-gpt-3-app-with-nextjs-react-and-github-copilot/

Codex (OpenAI)

OpenAI Codex is a fine-tuned GPT3-based LLM that generates code from text. In fact, Codex powers GitHub Copilot. Codex was trained on more than 150 GB of Python code that was obtained from more than 50 million GitHub repositories.

According to OpenAI, the primary purpose of Codex is to accelerate human programming, and it can complete almost 40% of requests. Codex tends to work quite well for generating code for solving simpler tasks. Navigate to the Codex home page to obtain more information: *https://openai.com/blog/ openai-codex*.

Apple GPT

In mid-2023, Apple announced Apple GPT, which is a competitor to ChatGPT from OpenAI. The actual release date was projected to be 2024. "Apple GPT" is the current name for a product that is intended to compete with Google Bard, OpenAI ChatGPT, and Microsoft Bing AI.

The LLM PaLM 2 powers Google Bard. GPT-4 powers ChatGPT as well as Bing Chat, whereas Ajax is what powers Apple GPT. Ajax is based on Jax from Google, and the name "Ajax" is a clever concatenation of "Apple" and "Jax".

PaLM-2

Pathways Language Model 2 (PaLM-2) is the successor to PaLM (circa 2022). PaLM-2 powers Bard, and it is also a direct competitor to GPT-4. By way of comparison, PaLM consists of 540 B parameters, and it is plausible that PaLM-2 is a larger LLM (details of the latter are undisclosed).

PaLM-2 provides four submodels called Gecko, Otter, Bison, and Unicorn (from smallest to largest). PaLM-2 was trained in more than 100 human languages, as well as programming languages such as Fortran. Moreover, PaLM-2 has been deployed to a plethora of Google products, including Gmail and YouTube.

Med-PaLM M

In addition to the four submodels listed above, Med-PaLM 2 (the successor to Med-PaLM) is an LLM that provides answers to medical questions, and it is accessible online at the following URL:

http://sites.research.google/med-palm/

The successor to Med-PaLM is Med-PaLM M. Details about this LLM are accessible at *https://arxiv.org/abs/2307.14334*.

The following is an article that provides a direct comparison of performance benchmarks for PaLM 2 and GPT-4:

https://www.makeuseof.com/google-palm-2-vs-openai-gpt-4/

PaLM-2 has a robust set of features, and it is definitely a significant competitor to GPT-4.

Claude 2

Anthropic created the LLM Claude 2, which can not only answer queries about specific topics, but also perform searches that involve multiple documents, summarize documents, create documents, and generate code.

Claude 2 is an improvement on Anthropic's predecessor Claude 1.3, and it can "ingest" entire books as well as generate code based on prompts from users. In fact, Claude 2 appears to be comparable with its rivals ChatGPT and GPT-4 in terms of competing functionality.

Furthermore, Claude 2 supports a context window of 100,000 tokens. Claude 2 was trained on data as recently as early 2023, whereas ChatGPT was trained on data up until 2021. However, Claude 2 cannot search the Web (unlike its competitor GPT-4). Anthropic will likely be accomplishing more with future releases of Claude 2.

LLAMA-2

Large Language Model Meta AI 2 (Llama 2) is an open source fine-tuned LLM from Meta. It was trained on only public data, and it has created a lot of excitement in the AI community. LlaMa-2 provides three models (7 B, 13 B, and 70 B parameters) that utilize more data during the pre-training step than numerous other LLMs. LlaMa-2 is optimized to provide faster inferences and also provides a longer context length (4 K) than other LLMs.

Moreover, the LlaMa-2-Chat LLM performs surprisingly well: in some cases, its quality is close to the quality of high-performing LLMs such ChatGPT and GPT-4. LlaMa-2 is more user-friendly and provides better results for writing text in comparison to GPT-4. However, GPT-4 is more adept for tasks such as generating code.

How to Download LlaMa-2

LlaMa-2 provides a permissive license for community use and commercial use, and Meta has made the code as well as the pre-trained models and the fine-tuned models publicly available.

There are several ways that you can download Llama-2. At the website from Meta, you will need to provide some information to gain access (name, country, and affiliation):

https://ai.meta.com/llama/

Another way to access demos of the 7 B, 13 B, and 70 B models is from the following links:

https://huggingface.co/spaces/huggingface-projects/llama-2-7b-chat

https://huggingface.co/spaces/huggingface-projects/llama-2-13b-chat

https://huggingface.co/spaces/ysharma/Explore_llamav2_with_TGI

Another way to access Llama-2 is from the following links:

https://huggingface.co/blog/llama2

https://github.com/facebookresearch/llama

https://ai.meta.com/research/publications/llama-2-open-foundation-and-fine-tuned-chat-models/

If you are interested in training LlaMa-2 on your laptop, more details for doing so are accessible at *https://blog.briankitano.com/llama-from-scratch/*.

LlaMa-2 Architecture Features

This section contains a high-level list of some of the important distinguishing features of LlaMa-2 (not discussed in this book), as shown here:

- decoder-only LLM
- better pre-training
- improved model architecture
- SwiGLU activation function
- different positional embeddings
- GQA (Grouped Query Attention)
- Ghost Attention (GAtt)
- RLHF and PPO
- BPE SentencePiece tokenizer
- modified normalization step

The majority of LLMs contain the layer normalization that is in the original transformer architecture. By contrast, LlaMA uses a simplified alternative that involves Root Mean Square Layer Normalization (RMSNorm). RMSNorm has yielded improved results for training stability as well as for generalization.

Although SwiGLU is computationally more expensive than the ReLU activation function that is part of the original transformer architecture, SwiGLU achieves better performance.

For a detailed description of how to fine-tune LlaMa-2 on three tasks, navigate to the following URL:

https://www.anyscale.com/blog/fine-tuning-llama-2-a-comprehensive-case-study-for-tailoring-models-to-unique-applications

Fine-Tuning LlaMa-2

Although Llama-2 is an improvement over its predecessor Llama, you can further improve the performance of Llama-2 by performing some fine-tuning of this LLM. See the following article for more information:

https://medium.com/@murtuza753/using-llama-2-0-faiss-and-langchain-for-question-answering-on-your-own-data-682241488476

The following article shows you how to fine-tune LlaMa-2 in a Google Colaboratory notebook:

https://towardsdatascience.com/fine-tune-your-own-llama-2-model-in-a-colab-notebook-df9823a04a32

The following article describes how to use MonsterAPI (also discussed in the article) to fine-tune Llama-2 in five steps:

https://blog.monsterapi.ai/how-to-fine-tune-llama-2-llm/

The following link describes how to access LlaMa-2 in Google Colaboratory:

https://levelup.gitconnected.com/harnessing-the-power-of-llama-2-using-google-colab-2e1dedc2d1d8

WHEN IS GPT-5 AVAILABLE?

As this book goes to print, there is no official information available regarding the status of GPT-5, which is to say that everything is speculative. In the early part of 2023, Sam Altman (CEO of OpenAI) remarked that there were "no official plans" for GPT-5.

However, during mid-2023, OpenAI filed a patent for GPT-5 in which there are some high-level details about the features of GPT-5. Some people have speculated that GPT-5 will be a more powerful version of GPT-4, and others suggest that filing a patent might be nothing more than securing the name GPT-5 by OpenAI.

Regardless of the motivation for filing a patent, there is a great deal of competition with GPT-4 from various companies. According to more recent speculation, it's possible that OpenAI will release GPT-5 toward the end of 2024. Regarding model sizes, recall that GPT-3 has 175 B parameters, and some speculate that GPT-4 has 10 trillion parameters, which would mean that GPT-4 is roughly 60 times larger than GPT-3. The same increase in scale for GPT-5 seems implausible because GPT-5 would then consist of 600 trillion parameters.

Another possibility is that GPT-4 is based on the MoE methodology, which involves multiple components. For instance, GPT-4 could be a combination of 8 components, each of which involves 220 million parameters, and therefore GPT-4 would consist of 1.76 trillion parameters.

Keep in mind that training LLMs such as GPT-4 is very costly and requires huge datasets for the pre-training step. Regardless of the eventual size of GPT-5, the training process could involve enormous costs.

SUMMARY

This chapter started with a discussion of ChatGPT from OpenAI and some of its features. In addition, you will learn about some competitors to ChatGPT, such as Claude 2 from Anthropic.

Next, you learned about GPT-4 from OpenAI, which powers ChatGPT, and some of its features. Then you learned about some competitors of GPT-4, such as LlaMa-2 (Meta) and Bard (Google).

## CHAPTER 2

CHATGPT AND PYTHON

This chapter contains examples of using ChatGPT to perform an eclectic mix of Python tasks, from creating a simple calculator to determining the probabilities involved in throwing two or more dice.

ChatGPT generated all the code samples in this chapter. Although the example of asyncio in Listing 2.10 executes with an error, ChatGPT provided debugging suggestions that eventually led to the successful execution of this code that is shown in Listing 2.11. The complete debugging "session" with ChatGPT is approximately three pages, and it is displayed in its entirety after Listing 2.10. This code sample shows you the remarkable capability of ChatGPT.

The first part of this chapter starts with an example of generating a simple numeric calculator that you can extend by providing additional functionality (such as support for trigonometric functions). This section also contains Python code for handling text files and scraping websites.

The second part of this chapter contains Python code for creating a basic chatbot as well as performing data visualization. In addition, you will learn how to generate random numbers in Pandas.

The third part of this chapter introduces you to Fibonacci numbers, object-oriented programming (OOP), asynchronous programming, and how to work with the requests library in Python.

The fourth part of this chapter shows you how to use the Python Imaging Library (PIL) for processing images and how to handle exceptions, as well as an introduction to generators and decorators in Python. The final section of this chapter shows you how to calculate the probability of obtaining a certain number when rolling two, three, or four fair dice.

As you will see, the ChatGPT prompts for generating the code samples in this chapter (and other chapters as well) are based on the following format:

```
"Please generate Python code for [specify a task] that
performs [specific features]."
```

Also keep in mind that the first few code samples contain the actual prompt for ChatGPT, after which you can easily infer the prompts for the subsequent code samples.

SIMPLE CALCULATOR

Listing 2.1 displays the content of `simple_calculator.py` that ChatGPT generated as a rudimentary calculator, based on the following prompt for ChatGPT:

```
"Please generate Python code for a simple calculator
that performs addition, subtraction, division, and
multiplication."
```

LISTING 2.1: simple_calculator.py

```python
def calculator(a, b, operation):
    if operation == 'add':
        return a + b
    elif operation == 'subtract':
        return a - b
    elif operation == 'multiply':
        return a * b
    elif operation == 'divide':
        if b == 0:
            return "Cannot divide by zero!"
        return a / b
    else:
        return "Invalid operation"

# Usage
result = calculator(5, 3, 'add')
print(result)  # Output: 8
```

Listing 2.1 starts with a Python function that processes two integers, a and b, as well as an arithmetic operator. The code consists of a sequence of if/elif statements that add, subtract, multiply, or divide the numbers a and b, provided that the value of the operator is for addition, subtraction, multiplication, and division, respectively. If the operator is not in this list, then a message is returned to the main part of the program. The final portion of Listing 2.1 invokes the `calculate()` function with the numbers 3 and 5 and the addition operator.

As you can see, there is no error checking to ensure that a and b are both numeric values, and there is no check for the operator to ensure that it always consists of lowercase letters. Launch the code in Listing 2.1, and you will see that its output is the value 8.

SIMPLE FILE HANDLING

Listing 2.2 displays the content of `file_handling.py` that ChatGPT generated to read content from a file and then write new content to a different file, based on the following prompt for ChatGPT:

```
"Please generate Python code in order to read the contents
of a text file and also write text to a file."
```

LISTING 2.2: file_handling.py

```
def read_file(file_path):
    with open(file_path, 'r') as file:
        return file.read()

def write_to_file(file_path, content):
    with open(file_path, 'w') as file:
        file.write(content)

# Usage
content = read_file('source.txt')
write_to_file('destination.txt', content)
```

Listing 2.2 starts with two Python functions `read_file()` and `write_to_file()` that read the contents of a file and write text to a file, respectively.

The function `read_file()` invokes the `open()` function to open a text file in read-only mode and then returns the contents of the file via the `file.read()` code snippet.

The function `write_to_file()` invokes the `open()` function to open a text file in write-only mode and then write the contents to the file. The final portion of Listing 2.2 invokes the `read_file()` function with the filename `source.txt` and then invokes the `write_to_file()` function with the contents of the file `source.txt`.

Notice several details about this code sample. First, there is no error handling to check if the path to the file `destination.txt` exists, or to handle the case where the path is valid, but the file does not exist. Second, the code does not check if the file `destination.txt` has write privileges.

Create a file called `source.txt`, and place some text in this file. Next, launch the code in Listing 2.2 and confirm that `destination.txt` contains the same text as the file `source.txt`.

SIMPLE WEB SCRAPING

Listing 2.3 displays the content of `web_scraping.py` that ChatGPT generated to perform Web scraping, based on the following prompt for ChatGPT:

```
"Please generate Python code for scraping the contents of a
Web page."
```

NOTE *Make sure you have installed the libraries* BeautifulSoup *and* requests, *which you can perform from the command line as follows:*

```
pip3 install bs4
pip3 install requests
```

LISTING 2.3: web_scraping.py

```python
import requests
from bs4 import BeautifulSoup

def scrape_titles(url):
    response = requests.get(url)
    soup = BeautifulSoup(response.content, 'html.parser')

    titles = []
    for title in soup.find_all('h2', class_='article-title'):
        titles.append(title.text)

    return titles

# Usage
# titles = scrape_titles('https://yourwebsite.com/articles')
# print(titles)
```

Listing 2.3 starts by importing requests and BeautifulSoup, followed by the function scrape_titles() that scrapes the contents of a given URL. Specifically, this function initializes the variable response with the result of invoking the get() method with a given URL. Next, this function initializes the variable soup with the parsed contents of response.content.

The second part of this function contains a loop that iterates through all the <h2> HTML tags that also have a class attribute equal to article-title. For each such item, the text of the item is appended to the Python variable titles, which is initialized as an empty Python list. When the loop has completed, the code returns the variable titles, which consists of titles listed on the website.

The final portion of Listing 2.3 contains a "commented out" code block that initializes the variable titles with the result, of invoking scrape_titles() with a fictional URL and then displaying the result. Replace the fictional URL with a valid URL, uncomment the final code snippets, and then check the generated output.

BASIC CHATBOT

Listing 2.4 displays the content of basic_chatbot.py that ChatGPT generated to perform Web scraping, based on the following prompt for ChatGPT:

```
"Please generate Python code for a rudimentary chatbot."
```

LISTING 2.4: basic_chatbot.py

```python
from bs4 import BeautifulSoup

def chatbot_response(text):
    responses = {
        'hello': 'Hi there!',
        'how are you': 'I am fine, thank you!',
        'bye': 'Goodbye!',
    }

    return responses.get(text.lower(), 'I am sorry, I do
not understand that.')

# Usage
response = chatbot_response('Hello')
print(response)  # Output: Hi there!
```

Listing 2.4 starts by importing `BeautifulSoup`, followed by the function `chatbot_responses()`, which initializes the variable `responses` as a Python dictionary. The final portion of this function issues a `return` statement that converts the variable text to lowercase, and then the value associated with this lowercase string in the `responses` dictionary. If the string is not found, then a disclaimer message is returned.

The final portion of Listing 2.4 invokes the function `chatbot_response()` with the string `Hello`, which is a key in the `responses` dictionary. Now launch the code in Listing 2.4, and you will see the output `Hi there!.`, which is the value associated with the key `Hello` in the `responses` dictionary.

BASIC DATA VISUALIZATION

Listing 2.5 displays the content of `basic_visualization.py` that ChatGPT generated to perform simple data visualization, based on the following prompt for ChatGPT:

```
"Please generate Python code that uses Matplotlib in order
to perform data visualization."
```

NOTE   *For this task, you need to have the* `matplotlib` *library installed as follows:*

```
pip3 install matplotlib
```

LISTING 2.5: basic_visualization.py

```python
import matplotlib.pyplot as plt

def plot_graph(x, y, title, x_label, y_label):
```

```
    plt.plot(x, y)
    plt.title(title)
    plt.xlabel(x_label)
    plt.ylabel(y_label)
    plt.grid(True)
    plt.show()

# Usage
x = [1, 2, 3, 4, 5]
y = [2, 4, 1, 3, 5]
plot_graph(x, y, 'Sample Line Graph', 'X-Axis', 'Y-Axis')
```

Listing 2.5 starts by importing `matplotlib.pyplot`, followed by the function `plot_graph()`, which plots a line graph with a grid background as well as labeled horizontal and vertical axes.

The next portion of Listing 2.5 initializes the Python lists x and y and passes them to the `plot_graph()` function, along with the strings `'Sample Line Graph'`, `'X-Axis'`, and `'Y-Axis'` for labels for the title, horizontal axis, and the vertical axis, respectively. Launch the code in Listing 2.5, and you will see the line graph in Figure 2.1.

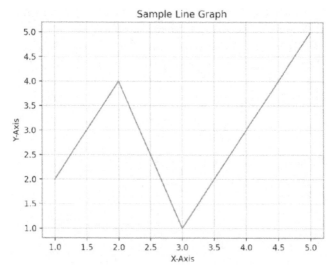

FIGURE 2.1 A line graph rendered via Matplotlib

BASIC PANDAS

Pandas is a powerful library for data manipulation. Be sure to install Pandas via the following command from the command line:

```
pip3 install pandas
```

Listing 2.6 displays the content of `basic_pandas.py` that ChatGPT generated to read the contents of a CSV file, and then compute the mean of a column in a subset of the rows of data.

LISTING 2.6: basic_pandas.py

```
import matplotlib.pyplot as plt
import pandas as pd

def process_data(file_path):
    # Load data from CSV
    data = pd.read_csv(file_path)

    # Filter rows where 'value' column is greater than 50
    filtered_data = data[data['value'] > 50]

    # Compute the mean of the 'value' column
    mean_value = filtered_data['value'].mean()

    return mean_value

# Usage
mean = process_data('data.csv')
print('mean:',mean)
```

Listing 2.6 starts with two `import` statements, followed by the `process_data()` function that populates the variable `data`, which is a Pandas data frame, with the contents of a CSV file.

The next portion of this function initializes the variable `filtered_data` with the rows for which the `value` feature (attribute) is greater than 50. The final portion of this function invokes the `mean()` method on the rows in the variable `filtered_data` and then returns this value.

The final portion of Listing 2.6 invokes the function `process_data()` with the file `data.csv`. Create this file with some data of your choice, making sure that there is a column with the label `value`. Launch the code in Listing 2.6, and you will see the average of the rows in which `value` is greater than 50.

GENERATE RANDOM DATA

In this section, you learn how to generate a list of random numbers and compute their mean and standard deviation. Listing 2.7 displays the content of `random_data_stats.py` that ChatGPT produced to generate a set of random numbers and then display the contents of those numbers, as well as the mean and standard deviation of those numbers.

LISTING 2.7: random_data_stats.py

```
import random
import statistics

def generate_statistics(n):
    # Generate n random numbers between 1 and 100
    numbers = [random.randint(1, 100) for _ in range(n)]

    # Compute mean and standard deviation
```

```
      mean = statistics.mean(numbers)
      std_dev = statistics.stdev(numbers)

      return numbers, mean, std_dev

# Usage
numbers, mean, std_dev = generate_statistics(100)
print(f"Numbers: {numbers}")
print(f"Mean: {mean}")
print(f"Standard Deviation: {std_dev}")
```

Listing 2.7 starts with two `import` statements, followed by the Python function `generate_statistics()` that populates the list `numbers` with a set of n randomly generated integers that are between 1 and 100.

The next portion of this function invokes the methods `mean()` and `stdev()` of the `statistics` library to initialize the variables `mean` and `std_dev` with the mean and standard deviation, respectively, of the integers in `numbers`. The final code snippet in this function returns `numbers`, `mean`, and `std_dev`.

The final portion of Listing 2.7 initializes the variables `numbers`, `mean`, and `std_dev` with the result that is returned by invoking `generate_statistics()` with the value 100 (which is the number of randomly generated numbers) and then displays their values. Launch the code in Listing 2.7, and you will see the following type of output (your output will be slightly different):

```
Numbers: [78, 41, 14, 67, 74, 90, 73, 2, 49, 22, 41, 86,
66, 62, 56, 73, 19, 38, 71, 8, 81, 38, 52, 80, 6, 52, 44,
48, 60, 87, 90, 43, 16, 46, 9, 65, 18, 22, 42, 45, 97, 19,
99, 17, 80, 47, 31, 12, 45, 35, 21, 26, 28, 88, 87, 93, 16,
19, 96, 16, 49, 29, 41, 25, 29, 39, 73, 45, 88, 17, 40, 5,
47, 29, 42, 71, 88, 93, 71, 89, 17, 96, 23, 92, 8, 71, 2,
56, 67, 87, 87, 38, 36, 51, 32, 89, 37, 59, 53, 86]
Mean: 50.43
Standard Deviation: 28.01127298323684
```

RECURSION: FIBONACCI NUMBERS

The Fibonacci sequence is a classic example of a problem that can be solved using recursion. Each Fibonacci number is the sum of the two preceding Fibonacci numbers.

Listing 2.8 displays the content of `fibonacci.py` that shows you how to compute the n-th Fibonacci number using recursion.

LISTING 2.8: fibonacci.py

```
def fibonacci(n):
    if n <= 1:
        return n
    return fibonacci(n-1) + fibonacci(n-2)
```

```
# Usage
result = fibonacci(10)
print(result)  # Output: 55
```

Listing 2.8 starts with the Python function `fibonacci()`, which contains the standard type of code for calculating Fibonacci numbers recursively. Launch the code in Listing 2.8, and you will see the value 55 as the output.

OBJECT ORIENTED PROGRAMMING

Listing 2.9 displays the content of `python_oop.py` that generates a rudimentary Python class that simulates two players who can score points.

LISTING 2.9: python_oop.py

```
class Player:
    def __init__(self, name):
        self.name = name
        self.score = 0

    def add_points(self, points):
        self.score += points

    def get_score(self):
        return self.score

# Usage
player = Player('Alice')
player.add_points(10)
print(f"{player.name}'s score: {player.get_score()}")
```

Listing 2.9 starts with the definition of the custom Python class `Player` that consists of three methods. The first method is the `__init__()` method, which acts as a constructor in Python. This method initializes the `name` and `score` variables, which represent a player's `name` and `score`, respectively.

The second method is `add_points()`, which increments a player's score with the value of the variable `points`. The third method is `get_score()`, which returns the value of the current player's score.

The final portion of Listing 2.9 initializes the variable `player` as an instance of the `Player` class with the name `Alice`, which initializes name and score as Alice and 0, respectively. The next code snippet invokes `add_points()` to add 10 points to Alice's score, and then displays the name and score values. Launch the code in Listing 2.9, and you will see the following output.

```
Alice's score: 10
```

ASYNCHRONOUS PROGRAMMING WITH ASYNCIO

This code sample demonstrates asynchronous programming by simulating two tasks running concurrently. Note that the first version of `async_example.py` was executed with an error, which you will see later in this section. ChatGPT provided several suggestions for addressing this problem, one of which resulted in a successful execution of the code.

The complete "dialogue" with ChatGPT to fix the issue is approximately 3 pages in length, and it appears after the explanation for Listing 2.10.

NOTE   *This example is best suited for Python 3.7+.*

LISTING 2.10: async_example.py

```
import asyncio

async def task_one():
    await asyncio.sleep(2)
    print("Task One Completed!")

async def task_two():
    await asyncio.sleep(1)
    print("Task Two Completed!")

# Usage
asyncio.run(asyncio.gather(task_one(), task_two()))
```

Asynchronous programming lets us handle tasks concurrently. In this example, `task_two()` completes before `task_one()` because the former has a the shorter sleep time than the latter, even though the latter is invoked before the former.

Listing 2.10 starts with an `import` statement, followed by the two functions `task_one()` and `task_two()`, which are invoked asynchronously. These functions invoke the `asyncio.sleep()` method with the values 2 and 3, respectively, which is the number of seconds that these functions will sleep before resuming execution. The code in Listing 2.10 was launched, and this was the output:

```
Traceback (most recent call last):
  File "async_example.py", line 14, in <module>
    loop.run_until_completed(task_one(), task_two())
AttributeError: '_UnixSelectorEventLoop' object has no
attribute 'run_until_completed'
```

Since this code sample was generated by ChatGPT, here is the subsequent interaction with ChatGPT.

ME: "I tried to execute your code sample and got an error [inserted the error message]."

ChatGPT:

```
This code seems correct. It defines two asynchronous
functions (task_one and task_two), and then uses asyncio.
run and asyncio.gather to run them concurrently.
```

The error message you provided, ValueError: a coroutine was expected, got <_GatheringFuture pending>, typically occurs when there's an issue related to not awaiting a coroutine or misusing asyncio.gather(). However, based on the code provided, I don't see these issues present.

To further assist, I have a few questions:

1. Are you using a version of Python that is 3.7 or newer? The asyncio.run() function was introduced in Python 3.7.
2. Is there any other code in async_example.py or another file that might be contributing to this error?
3. Are there any modifications or additions you made to the provided code before running it?

If the answer to the first question is "yes" and there are no other modifications, the code should run without the mentioned error. Otherwise, please provide additional details so I can assist further.

ME: "The answer to question #1 is 'yes', the answer to question #2 is 'no', and the answer to question #3 is 'no'."

ChatGPT:

Thank you for clarifying. Given your responses, the provided code should work correctly in a Python 3.7 or newer environment without modifications.

However, the error you're encountering is perplexing since the code appears to be correct. Here are some steps we can take to troubleshoot:

Python Interpreter: Ensure that you're running the code with the correct Python interpreter. Sometimes, systems have multiple Python versions installed, and there might be a mismatch. You can check the Python version by running python --version or python3 --version in the terminal or command prompt.

Virtual Environment: If you're using a virtual environment, ensure that it's activated and using Python 3.7 or newer.

Reinstallation: Occasionally, there might be inconsistencies or issues with the installed Python libraries. You can try reinstalling asyncio using pip:

```
pip install --upgrade --force-reinstall asyncio
```

After reinstalling, try running the code again.

```
External Interferences: Ensure that there aren't other
scripts or tools that might be interfering with the asyncio
module. For example, some third-party libraries or tools
might patch or modify the behavior of asyncio.

Code Execution: Try executing the code in a different
environment, such as an online Python compiler or a
different machine, to see if the error persists.

Minimal Reproduction: To isolate the issue, you can create
a new Python script with only the provided code and run it
to see if the error still occurs.
If after trying these steps the error persists, there might
be a deeper issue related to the specific environment or
system configuration. In that case, it would be helpful to
have more detailed information about the environment, any
error stack traces, or other relevant details to further
diagnose the problem.
```

ME: "I re-installed asyncio, but the same error occurs."

ChatGPT:

```
I'm sorry to hear that the issue persists. Let's take a
different approach to address it.

Given the error message you provided, it seems that
somewhere in the execution, the event loop expects a
coroutine but is getting a future object instead.

We can try using a different way to run the asynchronous
tasks and see if it resolves the error:
We can try using a different way to run the asynchronous
tasks and see if it resolves the error:
Explicitly Creating an Event Loop:

Instead of using asyncio.run(), we can try creating an
event loop explicitly and then use it to run the tasks.
```

At this point, ChatGPT provided two modified versions of the Python code in Listing 2.10, the first of which is shown in Listing 2.11. Since the code in Listing 2.11 did work correctly, the second modified version is not included.

LISTING 2.11: async_example2.py

```python
import asyncio

async def task_one():
    await asyncio.sleep(2)
    print("Task One Completed!")

async def task_two():
    await asyncio.sleep(1)
    print("Task Two Completed!")
```

```
# Create an event loop
loop = asyncio.get_event_loop()

# Run tasks using the created loop
try:
  loop.run_until_complete(asyncio.gather(task_one(), task_two()))
finally:
    loop.close()
```

Launch the code in Listing 2.11 by invoking the following command from the command line:

```
python3.7 async_example2.py
```

The following output is displayed, and there is a short pause before the second output line is shown:

```
Task Two Completed!
Task One Completed!
```

ME: "Solution #1 worked successfully! Thank you!"

ChatGPT:

```
You're welcome! I'm glad to hear that the first solution
worked successfully!

Using an explicit event loop can sometimes help bypass
issues or conflicts that might arise with the default
handling of asyncio.run().

If you have any more questions or need further assistance
with any other topic, feel free to ask. Happy coding!
```

WORKING WITH REQUESTS IN PYTHON

The `requests` library provides an intuitive way to send HTTP requests. Here, we fetch data from a given API URL and extract a specific piece of information using the key.

Listing 2.12 shows you the content of `requests_example.py` that demonstrates Web API Interaction using the Python `requests` library to fetch data from an API and extract specific information.

LISTING 2.12: *requests_example.py*

```
import requests

def fetch_api_data(api_url, key):
    response = requests.get(api_url)
    response.raise_for_status()
    data = response.json()
    return data.get(key, None)
```

```
# Usage
# replace the fictitious URL with a real URL:
# result = fetch_api_data('https://api.sampleendpoint.com/
data', 'desired_key')
# print(result)
```

Listing 2.12 starts with an `import` statement, and then the `fetch_api()` function retrieves the contents of the specified URL. This function invokes the `get()` method and then initializes the variable data with the JSON-formatted return string.

The next portion of Listing 2.12 initialed the variable `result` with the return value from invoking the function `fetch_api_data()`. You must replace the fictitious URL with a valid URL and a legitimate value for `desired_key` before you can launch the code.

IMAGE PROCESSING WITH PIL

The Python Imaging Library (PIL) allows for a vast array of image processing tasks. The code sample in this section performs several transformations on the file `sample3.png`.

Listing 2.13 shows you how to open an image, apply a grayscale filter, and save the result. In case you have not already done so, you need to install the Pillow library, a fork of PIL.

LISTING 2.13: *image_processing.py*

```
from PIL import Image, ImageFilter, ImageDraw

# Open an image
image_path = "sample3.png"
image = Image.open(image_path)

# 1. Convert the image to grayscale
grayscale_image = image.convert("L")
grayscale_image.show("Grayscale Image")

# 2. Apply a blur filter to the image
blurred_image = image.filter(ImageFilter.BLUR)
blurred_image.show("Blurred Image")

# 3. Rotate the image by 90 degrees
rotated_image = image.rotate(90)
rotated_image.show("Rotated Image")

# 4. Resize the image
new_dimensions = (300, 300)
resized_image = image.resize(new_dimensions)
resized_image.show("Resized Image")

# 5. Draw a red rectangle on the image
draw = ImageDraw.Draw(image)
draw.rectangle([(50, 50), (150, 150)], outline="red",
width=3)
image.show("Image with Rectangle")
```

```
# Save the processed images (optional)
grayscale_image.save("grayscale_output.jpg"w)
blurred_image.save("blurred_output.jpg")
rotated_image.save("rotated_output.jpg")
resized_image.save("resized_output.jpg")
image.save("rectangle_output.jpg")
```

Listing 2.13 starts with an `import` statement and then initializes the variable image with the result of invoking the `Image.open()` method with the file `sample3.png`. The next 5 code blocks apply transformations to generate 5 JPG files with the following names:

- `grayscale_output.jpg`
- `blurred_output.jpg`
- `rotated_output.jpg`
- `resized_output.jpg`
- `rectangle_output.jpg`

Launch the code in Listing 2.13, and you will see the preceding list of JPG files in your directory. Figure 2.2 displays the image that is generated by the first code block in Listing 2.13.

FIGURE 2.2 A gray scale image

Figure 2.3 displays the image that is generated by the second code block in Listing 2.13.

FIGURE 2.3 A blurred image

Figure 2.4 displays the image that is generated by the third code block in Listing 2.13.

FIGURE 2.4 A rotated image

Figure 2.5 displays the image that is generated by the fourth code block in Listing 2.13.

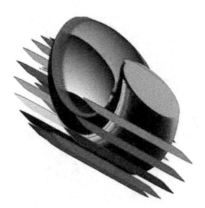

FIGURE 2.5 A resized image

Figure 2.6 displays the image that is generated by the fifth code block in Listing 2.13.

FIGURE 2.6 A rectangular image

Figure 2.7 displays the original image that Listing 2.13 used to generate the preceding images.

FIGURE 2.7 The original image

EXCEPTION HANDLING

Exception handling is crucial for robust programs. In this example, we define a custom exception and showcase its usage and handling. Listing 2.14 shows you how to perform custom exception handling in Python.

LISTING 2.14: exception_handling.py

```
class CustomError(Exception):
    pass

def raise_custom_exception(condition):
    if condition:
        raise CustomError("This is a custom exception!")

try:
    raise_custom_exception(True)
except CustomError as ce:
    print(f"Caught an exception: {ce}")
```

Listing 2.14 starts with the definition of the CustomError class that extends the Python Exception class. This class contains the raise_custom_ exception() function that raises an exception if the condition is true.

The second half of Listing 2.14 consists of a try/except block in which the custom exception is explicitly raised. The except portion of the code invokes print() to display a message. Launch the code in Listing 2.14, and you will see the following output.

```
Caught an exception: This is a custom exception!
```

GENERATORS IN PYTHON

Generators allow for lazy evaluation, producing values on-the-fly without storing the entire sequence in memory. Listing 2.15 shows you the content of fibonacci2.py that defines a generator that produces Fibonacci numbers in Python.

LISTING 2.15: fibonacci2.py

```
def fibonacci_generator(n):
    a, b = 0, 1
    for _ in range(n):
        yield a
        a, b = b, a + b

# Usage
for num in fibonacci_generator(10):
  print(num)
```

Listing 2.15 starts with the function fibonacci_generator(), which is a Python generator because of the placement of the yield statement. The details of Python generators are outside the scope of this book, but you can find online resources that go into detail regarding them.

The final portion of Listing 2.15 invokes the function fibonacci_generator() with the value 10 and then prints the returned value in a loop. Launch the code in Listing 2.15 and you will see the following output:

```
0
1
1
2
3
5
8
13
21
34
```

ROLL 7 OR 11 WITH TWO DICE

This section contains a dialogue with ChatGPT to determine the probability of rolling a 7 or an 11 with two balanced dice.

ME: "Suppose that I toss two fair dice and I win if the sum of the values is either 7 or 11. What is the probability that I win? Please provide an explanation."

ChatGPT:

```
Alright, let's break this down step by step.

There are two dice, and each die has 6 faces. So, when you
roll two dice, there are a total of 6×6=366×6=36 possible
outcomes, as each die can land on any of its 6 sides
independently of the other.
```

```
Now, let's consider the ways to get a sum of 7:
    Die 1 shows 1, Die 2 shows 6.
    Die 1 shows 2, Die 2 shows 5.
    Die 1 shows 3, Die 2 shows 4.
    Die 1 shows 4, Die 2 shows 3.
    Die 1 shows 5, Die 2 shows 2.
    Die 1 shows 6, Die 2 shows 1.
That's 6 ways to get a sum of 7.


Next, let's consider the ways to get a sum of 11:
    Die 1 shows 5, Die 2 shows 6.
    Die 1 shows 6, Die 2 shows 5.
That's 2 ways to get a sum of 11.


Combining both possibilities, there are a total of
6+2=86+2=8 ways to win.

So, the probability P of winning is given by:

P = (Number of winning outcomes)/(Total possible outcomes)

Let's compute the probability.

Given the number of winning outcomes as 8 and the total
possible outcomes when tossing two dice as 36, the
probability PP of winning is:

P = 8/36 = 2/9

Thus, the probability of winning is 2/9 or approximately
0.2222 (rounded to four decimal places).

In summary, when you toss two fair dice, the probability
that the sum of their values is either 7 or 11 is 2/9.
```

ROLL 7 OR 11 WITH THREE DICE

This section contains a dialogue with ChatGPT to determine the probability of rolling a 7 or an 11 with three balanced dice.

ME: "Suppose that I toss three fair dice and I win if the sum of the values is either 7 or 11. What is the probability that I win? Please provide an explanation."

ChatGPT:

```
When you roll three dice, each die can land on any of
its 6 sides independently of the others. So, there are a
total of 6×6×6=2166×6×6=216 possible outcomes.
```

Now, let's consider the ways to get a sum of 7 with three dice:

```
1, 1, 5
1, 2, 4
1, 3, 3
1, 4, 2
1, 5, 1
2, 1, 4
2, 2, 3
2, 3, 2
2, 4, 1
3, 1, 3
3, 2, 2
3, 3, 1
4, 1, 2
4, 2, 1
5, 1, 1
```

That's 15 ways to get a sum of 7 with three dice. Next, let's consider the ways to get a sum of 11:

```
2, 3, 6
2, 4, 5
2, 5, 4
2, 6, 3
3, 2, 6
3, 3, 5
3, 4, 4
3, 5, 3
3, 6, 2
4, 2, 5
4, 3, 4
4, 4, 3
4, 5, 2
5, 2, 4
5, 3, 3
5, 4, 2
6, 2, 3
6, 3, 2
```

That's 18 ways to get a sum of 11 with three dice. Combining both possibilities, there are a total of 15+18=3315+18=33 ways to win. So, the probability PP of winning is given by:

P = (Number of winning outcomes)/(Total possible outcomes)

Let's compute the probability. When you toss three fair dice, the probability that the sum of their values is either 7 or 11 is approximately 0.15280.1528 (rounded to four decimal places). To explain:

```
There are 15 possible combinations to get a sum of 7.
There are 18 possible combinations to get a sum of 11.

Combining both, there are 33 ways you can win out of
a total of 216 possible outcomes. Therefore, the winning
probability is 33/216 ≈ 0.152821633 ≈ 0.1528.

In summary, when you toss three dice, the probability of
their values summing up to either 7 or 11 is about 15.28%.
```

ROLL 7 OR 11 WITH FOUR DICE

This section contains a dialogue with ChatGPT to determine the probability of rolling a 7 or an 11 with four balanced dice.

ME: "Suppose that I toss three fair dice and I win if the sum of the values is either 7 or 11. What is the probability that I win? Please provide an explanation."

ChatGPT:

```
When dealing with four dice, calculating the probability
of their sum equating to either 7 or 11 involves
considering a lot more combinations than with fewer dice.
Let's tackle the problem step by step.

When you roll four dice, each die can land on any of its
6 sides independently of the others. So, the total possible
outcomes are 6×6×6×6=1,2966×6×6×6=1,296.

To determine the number of winning outcomes (sums of 7
or 11), we'll enumerate the combinations for each case:

We'll start by calculating all the combinations that
give a sum of 7.
Then, we'll calculate all the combinations that give a
sum of 11.
Finally, we'll sum up the counts from both cases and
divide by the total possible outcomes to get the
probability.

This computation can be quite involved, so we'll use a
programmatic approach to enumerate all the possible combinations
and count the ones that result in sums of 7 or 11.

When you toss four fair dice, the probability that the
sum of their values is either 7 or 11 is approximately
0.09570.0957 (rounded to four decimal places). To explain:

There are several possible combinations of four dice
that can sum up to either 7 or 11.
    Out of the 64=1,29664=1,296 possible outcomes when
tossing four dice, there are a specific number of
combinations that result in a sum of either 7 or 11.
```

Using a programmatic approach, we determined that the number of such combinations relative to the total possible outcomes yields a probability of about 9.57%.

In summary, when you toss four dice, the probability of their values summing up to either 7 or 11 is about 9.57%.

MEAN AND STANDARD DEVIATION

In this section, we calculate the mean and standard deviation of the numbers in the set S = {9,2,-8,17,4,37}. Listing 2.16 shows you the content of mean_std.py that ChatGPT generated to calculate the mean and standard deviation of a set of numbers.

LISTING 2.16: mean_std.py

```
import numpy as np

# Given set of numbers
S = [9, 2, -8, 17, 4, 37]

# Calculate mean and standard deviation
mean_S = np.mean(S)
std_dev_S = np.std(S)

print("mean_S    =",mean_S)
print("std_dev_S =",std_dev_S)
```

Listing 2.16 starts with an import statement and then initializes the set S with six numbers. The next code snippets initialize the variables mean_S and std_dev_S by invoking the methods mean() and std(), respectively, of the NumPy library. The final portion of Listing 2.16 displays the values of these variables. Launch the code in Listing 2.16, and you will see the following output:

```
mean_S    = 10.166666666666666
std_dev_S = 14.158821357098276
```

SUMMARY

This chapter contains Python-based solutions generated by ChatGPT to address a variety of tasks. The first set involved tasks such as creating a simple calculator, Web scraping, and file-based operations.

Then you learned about data visualization using a popular open-source Python-based library called Matplotlib. In addition, you learned how to use recursion to calculate Fibonacci numbers, followed by an example that uses a generator to calculate Fibonacci numbers.

You also saw a very interesting example of how to interact with ChatGPT in order to debug a code sample that was generated by ChatGPT in Listing 2.10 and Listing 2.11.

We discussed how to perform image processing in Python involving multiple transformations on a PNG file. We also saw how to define custom exception handlers in Python, as well as how to work with generators in Python.

You learned how to calculate probabilities of obtaining a given number by tossing 2, 3, or 4 well-balanced dice. Finally, you saw how to calculate the mean and the standard deviation of a set of numbers.

## CHAPTER 3

CHATGPT AND DATA VISUALIZATION

T his chapter contains examples of using ChatGPT to perform data visualization, such as creating charts and graphs based on datasets (e.g., the
Titanic dataset). ChatGPT generated all the code samples in this chapter via the Advanced Data Analysis (formerly known as Code Inspector) plugin.
ChatGPT also generated some of the accompanying text for the Python-based
code samples.

The first part of this chapter describes the process of uploading a dataset in
ChatGPT and then providing prompts for tasks, such as explaining the features
in a given dataset, generating visualizations, and downloading the curated dataset. You will also learn how to prompt ChatGPT to create and train a machine
learning model. The second part of this chapter contains examples of data visualization with Matplotlib, and the third part of this chapter contains examples
of data visualization with Seaborn.

As a reminder from Chapter 2, the ChatGPT prompts for generating the
code samples in this chapter (and other chapters as well) is based on the following format:

```
"Please generate Python code for [specify a task] that
performs [specific features]."
```

Also keep in mind that the first few code samples contain the actual prompt
for ChatGPT, after which you can easily infer the prompts for the subsequent
code samples.

WORKING WITH CHARTS AND GRAPHS

Each chart type has its unique strengths and is best suited for specific kinds of
data and analysis. The choice of chart often depends on the nature of the data and
the specific insights one wants to derive. This section contains multiple subsections
that provide information about an assortment of charts and graphs, as shown here:

- bar charts
- pie charts
- line graphs
- heat maps
- histograms
- box plots
- Pareto charts
- radar charts
- treemaps
- waterfall charts
- scatter plots

Each of the charts and graphs in the preceding list are discussed in the following subsections.

Bar Charts

Bar charts represent data with rectangular bars. The lengths of the bars are proportional to the values they represent. They can be vertical (column charts) or horizontal. An example of usage involves comparing the sales of different products in a store.

Some advantages of bar charts are as follows:

- easily interpretable and widely recognized
- can compare individual or multiple data series
- effective for displaying data that spans several categories

Some disadvantages of bar charts are listed here:

- not ideal for showing patterns or trends over time
- can become cluttered when comparing too many categories

Pie Charts

Pie charts represent data in a circular format, with individual sections (slices) showing categories' proportion to the whole. An example of usage involves representing the market share of different companies in an industry.

Some advantages of pie charts are listed here:

- simple visualization that shows part-to-whole relationships
- clearly indicate proportions
- effective when there are a limited number of categories

Some disadvantages of pie charts are listed here:

- not efficient for comparing individual categories
- can become ineffective and hard to interpret with too many slices
- do not show absolute values, only proportions

Line Graphs

Line graphs display data points connected by straight lines. They are used primarily to visualize values over a continuous interval or time period. An example of usage involves tracking a company's revenue growth over several years.

Some advantages of line graphs are listed here:

- effective for displaying trends over time
- can compare multiple data series on one graph
- clear visualization of data points and intervals

Some disadvantages of line graphs are listed here:

- not suitable for showing part-to-whole relationships
- can become cluttered when displaying too many data series
- requires a meaningful order of data points

Heat Maps

A heat map represents data in a matrix format, where individual values are depicted as colors. The color intensity usually represents the magnitude of the value. An example of usage involves visualizing website visitor activity on different parts of a Web page.

Some advantages of heat maps are listed here:

- quickly identifies patterns, correlations, and areas of concentration
- uses color effectively to convey information about magnitudes

Some disadvantages of heat maps are listed here:

- not suitable for detailed numerical analysis
- color choices are crucial; poor choices can result in faulty interpretation

Histograms

A histogram is a graphical representation of the distribution of a dataset. It is an estimate of the probability distribution of a continuous variable. An example of usage involves showing the distribution of ages in a population.

Some advantages of histograms are listed here:

- provide a visual interpretation of numerical data by indicating the number of data points that lie within a range of values
- can help identify data distribution patterns

Some disadvantages of histograms are listed here:

- do not show exact values
- number and width of bins can influence perception

Box Plots

Box plots (or box-and-whisker plots) represent a summary of a dataset using quartiles. The "box" shows the interquartile range, while the "whiskers" indicate variability outside the upper and lower quartiles. An example of usage involves comparing sales performances across different teams.

Some advantages of box plots are listed here:

- quickly visualize data spread and skewness
- identify outliers

Some disadvantages of box plots are listed here:

- not suitable for detailed distribution analysis
- do not show the frequency distribution of data

Pareto Charts

Pareto charts combine a bar chart and a line graph to represent the cumulative frequency of occurrences. These charts identify the most significant factors in a dataset. An example of usage involves identifying which product defects occur most frequently.

Some advantages of Pareto charts are listed here:

- efficiently highlight the most important factors in large datasets
- aid in prioritizing efforts

Some disadvantages of Pareto charts are listed here:

- limited to datasets where ranking and prioritization are relevant
- not suitable for showing relationships between data points

Radar Charts

Radar charts are a graphical method of displaying data in a 2D chart of three or more quantitative variables. The data points are plotted on axes that start from the center. An example of usage involves comparing the performance metrics of products.

Some advantages of radar charts are listed here:

- can compare multiple quantitative variables
- provide a visual overview of the data

Some disadvantages of radar charts are listed here:

- can become cluttered when comparing too many datasets
- hard to interpret with similar values

Treemaps

Treemaps display hierarchical data as nested rectangles. Each branch of the hierarchy is represented by colored rectangles. An example of usage involves visualizing storage usage on a computer.

Some advantages of treemaps are listed here:

- efficient use of space
- can represent multiple dimensions using size and color

Some disadvantages of treemaps are listed here:

- not suitable for datasets with large hierarchies
- can become hard to interpret

Waterfall Charts

Waterfall charts represent the cumulative effect of sequentially occurring positive or negative values. An example of usage involves visualizing how profit or revenue is affected by various factors.

Some advantages of waterfall charts are listed here:

- clearly visualize positive and negative sequential changes
- help in understanding the gradual transition from one data point to another

Some disadvantages of waterfall charts are listed here:

- limited to situations where understanding sequential changes is necessary
- can become confusing with too many data points

LINE PLOTS WITH MATPLOTLIB

In this section, we plot a simple line graph to visualize a trend. Listing 3.1 displays the content of `line_plots.py` that ChatGPT generated to render a line using Matplotlib, based on the following prompt for ChatGPT:

```
"Please generate Python code that uses Matplotlib to create
a line plot."
```

LISTING 3.1: line_plot.py

```
import matplotlib.pyplot as plt

def plot_line(x, y, title, x_label, y_label):
    plt.plot(x, y)
    plt.title(title)
```

```
      plt.xlabel(x_label)
      plt.ylabel(y_label)
      plt.grid(True)
      plt.show()

# Usage
x = [1, 2, 3, 4, 5]
y = [2, 4, 1, 3, 5]
plot_line(x, y, 'Sample Line Graph', 'X-Axis', 'Y-Axis')
```

Listing 3.1 starts with an `import` statement and then defines the function `plot_line()`, which renders a line plot. Matplotlib has the `plot()` function, which provides a straightforward way to create line graphs. In this function, we visualize a trend across the x and y axes.

The next portion of code initializes the Python lists x and y and then invokes `plot_line()` with three strings that are the values for the title, the horizontal axis, and the vertical axis. Figure 3.1 shows the output from launching the code in Listing 3.1.

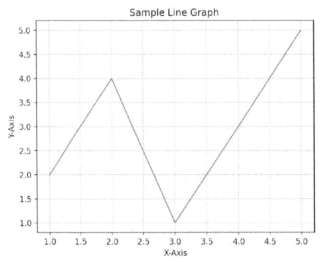

FIGURE 3.1 A line plot created with Matplotlib

A PIE CHART USING MATPLOTLIB

Pie charts are ideal for displaying proportional data among categories. The pie function from Matplotlib provides an easy way to achieve this. Listing 3.2 displays the content of `pie_chart1.py` that ChatGPT generated to render a line using Matplotlib, based on the following prompt for ChatGPT:

"Please generate Python code that uses Matplotlib in order to generate a pie chart."

LISTING 3.2: pie_chart1.py

```
import matplotlib.pyplot as plt

def plot_pie(labels, sizes, title):
    plt.pie(sizes, labels=labels, autopct='%1.1f%%',
startangle=140)
    plt.title(title)
    plt.axis('equal')   # Equal aspect ratio ensures the pie
is drawn as a circle.
    plt.show()

# Usage
labels = ['A', 'B', 'C']
sizes = [215, 130, 245]
plot_pie(labels, sizes, 'Sample Pie Chart')
```

Listing 3.2 starts in a similar fashion as Listing 3.1, except that the plot_Pie() function for generating a pie chart is created. The next portion of Listing 3.2 initializes the Python lists labels and sizes and invokes the function plot_pie(). A string is invoked that is displayed as the title of the pie chart. Figure 3.2 displays the pie chart that is rendered by launching the code in Listing 3.2.

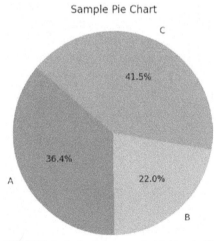

FIGURE 3.2: A pie chart created with Matplotlib

BOX-AND-WHISKER PLOTS USING MATPLOTLIB

Box plots, or box-and-whisker plots, provide a summary of the distribution of data, highlighting the central tendency, variability, and presence of outliers. They can be particularly useful for comparing distributions across different groups. These plots display the distribution of data based on the minimum, first quartile, median, third quartile, and maximum.

Listing 3.3 displays the content of boxplot1.py that ChatGPT generated to render a box plot using Seaborn, based on the following prompt for ChatGPT:

```
"Please generate Python code that uses Matplotlib to
generate a box plot."
```

LISTING 3.3: boxplot1.py

```python
import matplotlib.pyplot as plt
import seaborn as sns

import matplotlib.pyplot as plt

def plot_box(data, column):
    plt.boxplot(data[column])
    plt.show()

# Usage
data = sns.load_dataset("iris")
plot_box(data, "sepal_length")
```

Listing 3.3 contains three import statements followed by the plot_box() function that generated a box plot. The next portion of Listing 3.3 initializes the variable data with the contents of the Seaborn built-in iris dataset, and then invokes plot_box() with data and a string that specifies the feature (column) to use when rendering a box plot. Figure 3.3 shows the box plot that is rendered by launching the code in Listing 3.3.

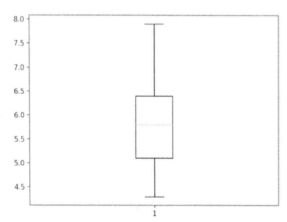

FIGURE 3.3: A box plot created with Matplotlib

TIME SERIES VISUALIZATION WITH MATPLOTLIB

Time series data, where observations are taken at regular time intervals, can be visualized using line plots. This enables analysts to discern trends, patterns, and anomalies.

We plot time series data to understand trends over time. Listing 3.4 displays the content of time_series.py that ChatGPT generated to render a time series using Matplotlib, based on the following prompt for ChatGPT:

```
"Please generate Python code that uses Matplotlib to
display time series data."
```

LISTING 3.4: time_series.py

```python
import matplotlib.pyplot as plt

import pandas as pd

def plot_time_series(dates, values, title):
    plt.figure(figsize=(10, 5))
    plt.plot(dates, values)
    plt.title(title)
    plt.xlabel('Date')
    plt.ylabel('Value')
    plt.tight_layout()
    plt.show()

# Usage
dates = pd.date_range(start="2021-01-01", periods=10,
freq='D')
values = [x**1.5 for x in range(10)]
plot_time_series(dates, values, 'Sample Time Series Data')
```

Figure 3.4 displays the time series that is rendered by launching the code in Listing 3.10.

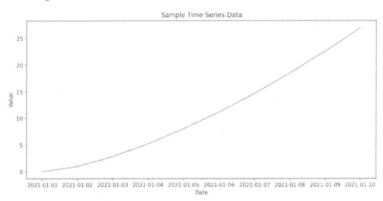

FIGURE 3.4: A time series created with Matplotlib

STACKED BAR CHARTS WITH MATPLOTLIB

Stacked bar charts allow for the representation of subgroups in each category, giving a sense of the total size across categories and the subgroup distributions within them.

Listing 3.5 displays the content of `stacked_bar_charts.py` that ChatGPT generated to render stacked bar charts using Matplotlib, based on the following prompt for ChatGPT:

```
"Please generate Python code for a simple calculator
that performs addition, subtraction, division, and
multiplication."
```

LISTING 3.5: stacked_bar_charts.py

```python
import matplotlib.pyplot as plt
import numpy as np

def plot_stacked_bar(data, labels, categories):
    cum_size = np.zeros(len(categories))

    for i, label in enumerate(labels):
        plt.bar(categories, data[label], bottom=cum_size,
label=label)
        cum_size += data[label]

    plt.legend()
    plt.show()

# Usage
data = {
    'A': [10, 15, 20],
    'B': [5, 10, 5]
}
labels = ['A', 'B']
categories = ['Category 1', 'Category 2', 'Category 3']
plot_stacked_bar(data, labels, categories)
```

Figure 3.5 shows the stacked bar charts that are rendered by launching the code in Listing 3.5.

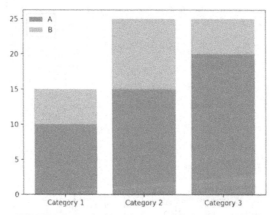

FIGURE 3.5: Stacked bar charts rendered with Matplotlib

DONUT CHARTS USING MATPLOTLIB

Donut charts are a variation of pie charts. The hollow center can be used for additional annotations or just to provide a different aesthetic. These charts represent data proportionally among categories, similar to a pie chart but with a hollow center. Listing 3.6 displays the content of donut_charts.py that ChatGPT generated to render a donut chart using Matplotlib.

LISTING 3.6: donut_charts.py

```
import matplotlib.pyplot as plt

def plot_donut_chart(sizes, labels, title, hole_size=0.3):
    fig, ax = plt.subplots()
    ax.pie(sizes, labels=labels, autopct='%1.1f%%',
startangle=90, wedgeprops=dict(width=hole_size))
    ax.axis('equal')
    plt.title(title)
    plt.show()

# Usage
labels = ['A', 'B', 'C']
sizes = [215, 130, 245]
plot_donut_chart(sizes, labels, 'Sample Donut Chart')
```

Figure 3.6 shows the donut chart that is rendered by launching the code in Listing 3.13.

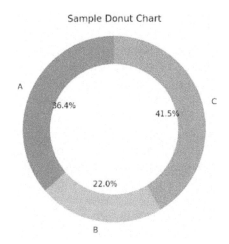

FIGURE 3.6: A donut chart rendered by Matplotlib

3D SURFACE PLOTS WITH MATPLOTLIB

3D surface plots are used for visualizing functions with two variables. They can reveal intricate patterns and relationships in the data. Listing 3.7 displays the content of `3d_surface.py` that ChatGPT generated to render a 3D surface using `mpl_toolkits`.

Incidentally, if you encounter issues with `mpl_toolkits`, please read the following post that contains useful information:

https://stackoverflow.com/questions/37661119/python-mpl-toolkits-installation-issue

LISTING 3.7: 3d_surface.py

```python
import matplotlib.pyplot as plt
import numpy as np

def plot_3d_surface(x, y, z):
    fig = plt.figure()
    ax = fig.add_subplot(111, projection='3d')
    ax.plot_surface(x, y, z, cmap='viridis')
    plt.show()

# Usage
x = np.linspace(-5, 5, 50)
y = np.linspace(-5, 5, 50)
x, y = np.meshgrid(x, y)
z = np.sin(np.sqrt(x**2 + y**2))
plot_3d_surface(x, y, z)
```

Listing 3.7 starts with two `import` statements, followed by the `plot_3d_surface()` function that renders a 3D plot. The second half of Listing 3.7 initializes the variables x and y via the NumPy function `linspace()`, which partitions an interval into a set of equally-sized subintervals.

For example, the code snippet `np.linspace(-5, 5, 50)` divides the interval `[-5,5]` into 50 equally spaced points, which means that there are 49 intervals of equal width. You can persuade yourself that this is true by replacing 50 with 3: the result is the left endpoint −5, the midpoint, and the right endpoint 5, which creates 2 (=3−1) intervals.

The next code snippet updates x and y with the result of invoking the `meshgrid()` function in NumPy, after which z is defined as the trigonometric sine function applied to the number that equals the distance of the point (x, y) from the origin. The latter number is monotonically increasing as the point (x, y) shifts away from the origin, and z is the sine of that distance, which is a periodic function. As a result, you will see a rolling wave-like effect.

The final code snippet in Listing 3.7 invokes the function `plot_3d_surface()` with the values contained in the variables x, y, and z. Launch the code in Listing 3.7, and you will see the 3D surface that is shown in Figure 3.7.

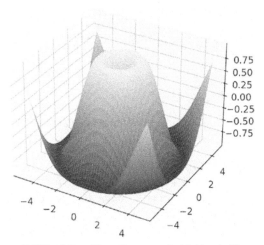

FIGURE 3.7: A 3D surface created with Matplotlib

RADIAL OR SPIDER CHARTS WITH MATPLOTLIB

Radial (or spider) charts are used to visualize multivariate data in the form of a two-dimensional chart of three or more quantitative variables. Each variable is represented on a separate axis that starts from the center of the chart. These charts allow us to compare multiple quantitative variables.

Listing 3.8 displays the content of `radial_charts.py` that ChatGPT generated to render radial charts using Matplotlib.

LISTING 3.8: radial_charts.py

```
import matplotlib.pyplot as plt
import numpy as np

def plot_spider_chart(values, categories, title):
    angles = np.linspace(0, 2 * np.pi, len(categories),
endpoint=False).tolist()
    values += values[:1]
    angles += angles[:1]

    fig, ax = plt.subplots(figsize=(6, 6), subplot_
kw=dict(polar=True))
    ax.fill(angles, values, color='blue', alpha=0.25)
    ax.set_yticklabels([])

# the following snippet causes an error:
# ax.set_xticks(angles)
# the following snippet is correct:
ax.set_xticks(angles[:-1])   # Exclude the last angle since
it's cyclic
```

```
    ax.set_xticklabels(categories)

    plt.title(title, size=20, color="blue", y=1.1)
    plt.show()

# Usage
categories = ["A", "B", "C", "D"]
values = [50, 30, 60, 40]
plot_spider_chart(values, categories, 'Sample Spider
Chart')
```

Listing 3.8 starts with two `import` statements, followed by the `plot_spider_chart()` function that renders a radial chart. The second portion of Listing 3.8 initializes the variables `categories` and `values` as two Python lists and then invokes the function `plot_spider_chart()` with the variables `categories`, `values`, and a text string for the title of the plot. Figure 3.8 shows the radial chart that is rendered by launching the code in Listing 3.8.

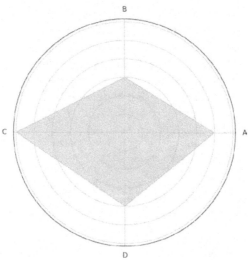

FIGURE 3.8: A radial chart created with Matplotlib

Here is one more detail that will help you with debugging the code that ChatGPT generates. Let's look at the code block in bold in Listing 3.8:

```
# the following snippet causes an error:
# ax.set_xticks(angles)
# the following snippet is correct:
ax.set_xticks(angles[:-1])   # Exclude the last angle since
it's cyclic
```

If you reverse the order of the two code snippets, the code will not work correctly. Here is the "conversation" with ChatGPT to ask for a solution.

ME: "I uploaded radial_charts.py that contains code that you wrote for me. However, this code results in this error: ValueError: The number of FixedLocator locations (5), usually from a call to set_ticks, does not match the number of ticklabels (4). Can you provide a solution?"

ChatGPT:

Thank you for providing the radial_charts.py file. Let's start by reading its content to understand the structure and context of the code. After that, I'll analyze the potential causes of the mentioned error and offer a solution.

The provided radial_charts.py file contains a function, plot_spider_chart, which is designed to plot a spider (or radar) chart using given values and categories.

Based on the error you reported and the code's structure, the issue likely arises from the mismatch between the number of tick locations (set by ax.set_xticks(angles)) and the number of tick labels (set by ax.set_xticklabels(categories)).

To address this, I'll ensure that the number of tick locations matches the number of tick labels. Let's proceed to make this adjustment and provide a corrected version of the function.

ME: "This works correctly now! Thank you for your help!"

ChatGPT:

You're welcome! I'm glad to hear it's working as expected now. If you have any more questions or need further assistance in the future, don't hesitate to reach out. Happy coding!

MATPLOTLIB'S CONTOUR PLOTS

Contour plots help visualize three-dimensional data in two dimensions using contour lines. Each contour line represents points of equal value.

Listing 3.9 displays the content of contour_lines.py that ChatGPT generated to render contour lines using Matplotlib.

LISTING 3.9: contour_lines.py

```
import matplotlib.pyplot as plt
import numpy as np

def plot_contour(x, y, z):
    plt.contourf(x, y, z, 20, cmap='viridis')
    plt.colorbar()
    plt.show()
```

```
# Usage
x = np.linspace(-5, 5, 50)
y = np.linspace(-5, 5, 50)
x, y = np.meshgrid(x, y)
z = np.sin(np.sqrt(x**2 + y**2))
plot_contour(x, y, z)
```

Listing 3.9 contains two `import` statements. Then, the function `plot_contour()` is defined, which renders the contour lines for the code sample. Note that the second part of Listing 3.9 is virtually identical to the code in the second half of Listing 3.7. Figure 3.9 shows the contour plot that is rendered by launching the code in Listing 3.9.

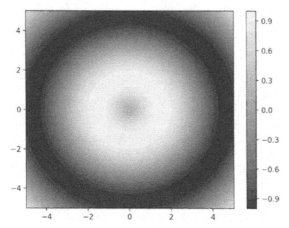

FIGURE 3.9: A contour plot created with Matplotlib

STREAM PLOTS FOR VECTOR FIELDS

Stream plots are used for displaying vector fields, like wind patterns. They provide a snapshot of the flow trajectories and can be color-coded for scalar data. Stream plots can visualize a vector field as streamlines.

Listing 3.10 displays the content of `stream_plot.py` that ChatGPT generated to render a stream plot using Seaborn.

LISTING 3.10: stream_plot.py

```
import matplotlib.pyplot as plt
import seaborn as sns
import numpy as np

def plot_streamplot(x, y, u, v):
    plt.streamplot(x, y, u, v, density=1)
    plt.show()

# Usage
x = np.linspace(-5, 5, 10)
y = np.linspace(-5, 5, 10)
```

```
# this causes an error:
# y, x = np.meshgrid(y, x)
# this works correctly:
x, y = np.meshgrid(x, y)

u = -1 - x**2 + y
v = 1 + x - y**2
plot_streamplot(x, y, u, v)
```

Figure 3.18 shows the stream plot that is rendered by launching the code in Listing 3.10.

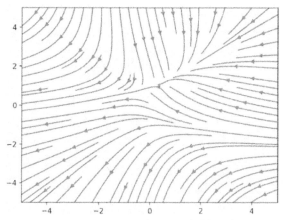

FIGURE 3.10: A stream plot created with Seaborn

The initial code in Listing 3.10 from ChatGPT did not work correctly, so I asked ChatGPT to provide a solution during the following "dialog."

ME: "I uploaded `stream_plot.py` *that contains code that you wrote for me. This code results in the following error: ValueError: The rows of 'x' must be equal. Can you provide a solution?"*

ChatGPT:

```
The shapes of the arrays x, y, u, and v are all (10,10),
which means they are consistent in terms of dimensions.

The error message "ValueError: The rows of 'x' must be
equal" suggests that there might be an issue with the values
within the rows of the x array, rather than its shape.

The line y, x = np.meshgrid(y, x) swaps the original x and
y arrays. This might be causing inconsistencies in the rows
of the x array.

To address the error, I'll modify the meshgrid creation and
ensure the x and y arrays are correctly initialized. Let's
make the necessary adjustments.
```

ME: "This works! Thanks for your help!"

ChatGPT:

```
You're welcome! I'm glad to hear it's working as expected now.
If you have any more questions or need further assistance in
the future, don't hesitate to reach out. Happy coding!
```

QUIVER PLOTS FOR VECTOR FIELDS

Quiver plots are useful for representing vector fields, showing both the direction and magnitude of vectors. For instance, they can be utilized in physics to show electric fields or fluid flow directions. They help visualize the direction and magnitude of vectors.

Listing 3.11 displays the content of `quiver_plot.py` that ChatGPT generated to render a quiver plot using Matplotlib.

LISTING 3.11: quiver_plot.py

```python
import matplotlib.pyplot as plt
import numpy as np

def plot_quiver(x, y, u, v):
    plt.quiver(x, y, u, v, scale=20)
    plt.show()

# Usage
x, y = np.meshgrid(np.arange(0, 2 * np.pi, .2),
np.arange(0, 2 * np.pi, .2))
u = np.sin(x)
v = np.cos(y)
plot_quiver(x, y, u, v)
```

Figure 3.11 shows the quiver plot that is rendered by launching the code in Listing 3.11.

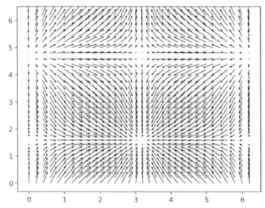

FIGURE 3.11: A quiver plot created with Matplotlib

POLAR PLOTS

Polar plots (or radial plots) are suitable for displaying multivariate data in a two-dimensional chart where the variables are represented on axes starting from the same point. They are useful for viewing patterns in data based on angles and magnitudes.

Listing 3.12 displays the content of `polar_plots.py` that ChatGPT generated to render polar plots using Matplotlib.

LISTING 3.12: polar_plots.py

```python
import matplotlib.pyplot as plt
import numpy as np

def plot_polar(theta, radii, title=""):
    plt.figure(figsize=(8, 4))
    ax = plt.subplot(111, projection='polar')
    ax.plot(theta, radii)
    ax.set_title(title)
    plt.show()
# Usage
theta = np.linspace(0, 2 * np.pi, 100)
radii = np.abs(np.sin(theta) * 2)
plot_polar(theta, radii, "Sample Polar Plot")
```

Figure 3.12 displays the polar plot that is rendered by launching the code in Listing 3.12.

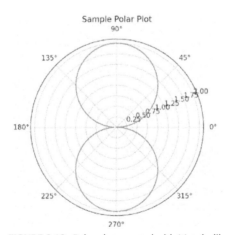

FIGURE 3.12: Polar plots created with Matplotlib

BAR CHARTS WITH SEABORN

Seaborn provides a higher-level interface for Matplotlib, making the creation of stylish plots possible. The code sample in this section involves bar charts, which are useful because they help visualize data across different categories.

Seaborn works best when integrated with Pandas.

Listing 3.13 displays the content of `bar_chart1.py` that `ChatGPT` generated to create a bar chart using Seaborn.

LISTING 3.13: bar_chart1.py

```
import matplotlib.pyplot as plt
import seaborn as sns
import pandas as pd

def plot_bar(data, x_col, y_col):
    sns.barplot(x=x_col, y=y_col, data=data)
    plt.show()

# Usage
data = pd.DataFrame({
    'Category': ['A', 'B', 'C'],
    'Values': [10, 20, 15]
})
plot_bar(data, 'Category', 'Values')
```

Listing 3.13 starts with three `import` statements, followed by the function `plot_bar()`, which renders the bar chart. The second half of Listing 3.13 initializes the Pandas data frame data and then invokes `plot_bar()` with data and a string for labeling the horizontal axis and another string for labeling the vertical axis. Figure 3.13 shows the bar chart that is rendered by launching the code in Listing 3.13.

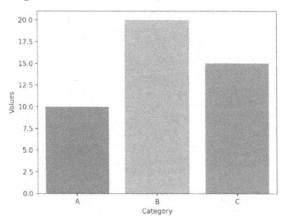

FIGURE 3.13: A bar chart created with Seaborn

SCATTER PLOTS WITH REGRESSION LINES USING SEABORN

Scatter plots can be used to display data points and a regression line to understand relationships. Listing 3.14 displays the content of `scatter_plot.py` that ChatGPT generated to render a scatter plot using Seaborn.

LISTING 3.14: scatter_plot.py

```
import matplotlib.pyplot as plt
import pandas as pd
import seaborn as sns

def plot_scatter_with_regression(data, x_col, y_col):
    sns.regplot(x=x_col, y=y_col, data=data)
    plt.show()

# Usage
data = pd.DataFrame({
    'X_Values': [10, 20, 30, 40, 50],
    'Y_Values': [15, 25, 35, 45, 55]
})
plot_scatter_with_regression(data, 'X_Values', 'Y_Values')
```

Scatter plots are useful for visualizing relationships between two variables. Seaborn has a regplot() function that not only plots the data points, but also fits a regression line.

Listing 3.14 starts with three import statements and the plot_scatter_with_regression() function that renders the scatter plot. The second half of Listing 3.13 initializes the Pandas data frame data and then invokes plot_scattter_with_regression() with the variable data. Figure 3.14 displays the scatter plot that is rendered by launching the code in Listing 3.14.

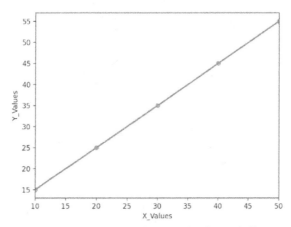

FIGURE 3.14: A scatter plot created with Matplotlib

HEATMAPS FOR A CORRELATION MATRIX WITH SEABORN

Heatmaps are powerful for representing matrices of data, with colors indicating magnitudes. A common use case is visualizing correlation matrices, which help in understanding relationships among different variables.

As an example, Listing 3.15 displays the content of heatmap1.py that ChatGPT generated to render a heat map using Matplotlib.

LISTING 3.15: heatmap1.py

```
import matplotlib.pyplot as plt
import pandas as pd
import seaborn as sns

def plot_heatmap(data):
    correlation_matrix = data.corr()
    sns.heatmap(correlation_matrix, annot=True,
cmap='coolwarm')
    plt.show()

# Usage
data = pd.DataFrame({
    'A': [1, 2, 3, 4, 5],
    'B': [5, 4, 3, 2, 1],
    'C': [2, 3, 4, 5, 6]
})
plot_heatmap(data)
```

Listing 3.15 starts with three `import` statements and the `plot_heatmap()` function that renders the heat map. The second half of Listing 3.15 initializes the Pandas data frame data and then invokes `plot_heatmap()` with the variable `data`. Figure 3.15 shows the heat map that is rendered by launching the code in Listing 3.15.

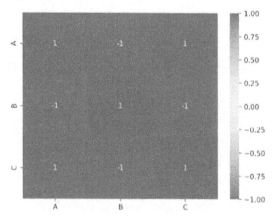

FIGURE 3.15: A heat map created with Matplotlib

HISTOGRAMS WITH SEABORN

Histograms are powerful tools for visualizing the distribution of data. Seaborn's `histplot()` function provides a way to easily generate histograms with additional features like the kernel density estimation.

Listing 3.16 displays the content of `histogram1.py` that ChatGPT generated to render a histogram using Seaborn.

LISTING 3.16: histogram1.py

```
import matplotlib.pyplot as plt
import seaborn as sns

def plot_histogram(data, column, bins=10):
    sns.histplot(data[column], bins=bins)
    plt.show()

# Usage
data = sns.load_dataset("iris")
plot_histogram(data, "sepal_length")
```

Listing 3.16 starts with two `import` statements and the `plot_histo-gram()` function that renders the histogram. The second half of Listing 3.16 initializes the Pandas data frame data with the contents of the Seaborn built-in dataset `iris`, and then invokes `plot_histogram()` with the variable data. Figure 3.16 shows the heat map for the `Iris` dataset that is rendered by launching the code in Listing 3.16.

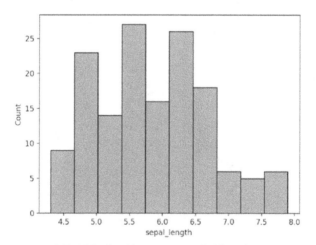

FIGURE 3.16: A histogram created with Seaborn

VIOLIN PLOTS WITH SEABORN

Violin plots offer a deeper understanding of the distribution of data. They combine the characteristics of box plots and histograms, showing the probability density of the data at different values.

Here, we combine aspects of box plots and histograms to provide rich descriptions of data distributions. Listing 3.17 displays the content of `violin_plots.py` that ChatGPT generated to render a violin plot using Seaborn.

LISTING 3.17: violin_plots.py

```
import seaborn as sns

def plot_violin(data, x_col, y_col):
    sns.violinplot(x=x_col, y=y_col, data=data)
    plt.show()

# Usage
data = sns.load_dataset("iris")
plot_violin(data, "species", "sepal_length")
```

Listing 3.17 starts with one `import` statement and the `plot_violin()` function, which renders the violin plot. The second half of Listing 3.17 initializes the Pandas data frame data and then initializes it with the contents of the Seaborn built-in dataset `iris`. It then invokes `plot_violin()` with the variable `data`. Figure 3.17 shows the violin plot that is rendered by launching the code in Listing 3.8.

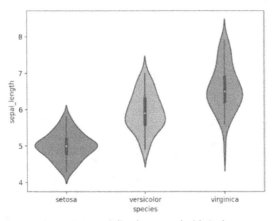

FIGURE 3.17: A violin plot created with Seaborn

PAIR PLOTS USING SEABORN

When dealing with datasets having multiple features, it is often helpful to visualize the pairwise relationships between features. Seaborn has a `pairplot()` function that generates a matrix of scatter plots, allowing for the exploration of such relationships.

Listing 3.18 displays the content of `pair_plots.py` that ChatGPT generated to render a pair plot using Matplotlib.

LISTING 3.18: pair_plots.py

```
import matplotlib.pyplot as plt
import seaborn as sns
```

```
def plot_pairplot(data):
    sns.pairplot(data)
    plt.show()

# Usage
data = sns.load_dataset("iris")
plot_pairplot(data)
```

Listing 3.18 starts with two `import` statements and the `plot_pairplot()` function that renders the pair plot. The second part of Listing 3.18 initializes the Pandas data frame data with the contents of the Seaborn built-in dataset `iris`, and then invokes `plot_pair()` with the variable `data`. Figure 3.18 shows the pair plot that is rendered by launching the code in Listing 3.18.

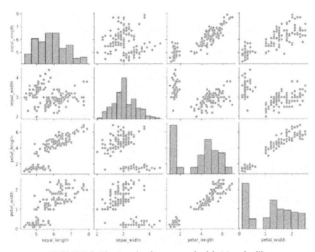

FIGURE 3.18: A pair plot created with Matplotlib

FACET GRIDS WITH SEABORN

Facet grids are a way to visualize the data distribution across several subplots based on a categorical variable. Each facet (subplot) represents a category. Listing 3.19 displays the content of `facet_grids.py` that ChatGPT generated to create and render multiple plots segmented by categories.

LISTING 3.19: *facet_grids.py*

```
import matplotlib.pyplot as plt
import seaborn as sns

def plot_facetgrid(data, x_col, y_col, facet_col):
    g = sns.FacetGrid(data, col=facet_col)
    g.map(sns.scatterplot, x_col, y_col)
    g.add_legend()
    plt.show()
```

```
# Usage
data = sns.load_dataset("iris")
plot_facetgrid(data, "sepal_length", "sepal_width",
"species")
```

Listing 3.19 starts with two `import` statements and the `plot_facet-grid()` function that renders the facets. The second part of Listing 3.19 initializes the Pandas DataFrame data with the contents of the Seaborn built-in dataset `iris`, and then invokes `plot_pair()` with the variable data. Figure 3.19 shows the facet grids rendered by launching the code in Listing 3.19.

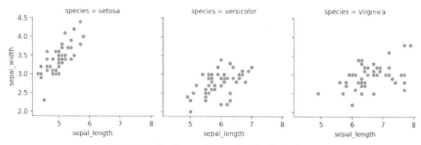

FIGURE 3.19: Facet grids rendered with Seaborn

HIERARCHICAL CLUSTERING

Seaborn's `clustermap` is a 2D matrix dataset representation where both rows and columns are hierarchically clustered. This allows patterns to emerge from complex datasets and allows for the visualization of hierarchically clustered relationships in a heatmap format.

LISTING 3.20: cluster_map.py

```
import matplotlib.pyplot as plt
import seaborn as sns

def plot_clustermap(data):
    sns.clustermap(data, method='average', cmap='coolwarm')
    plt.show()

# Usage
data = sns.load_dataset("iris").drop("species", axis=1)
plot_clustermap(data)
```

Listing 3.20 starts with two `import` statements and the `plot_clustermap()` function that renders the cluster map. The second part of Listing 3.20 initializes the Pandas DataFrame data with the contents of the Seaborn built-in dataset `iris`, and then invokes `plot_pair()` with the variable `data`. Figure 3.20 displays the cluster map that is rendered by launching the code in Listing 3.20.

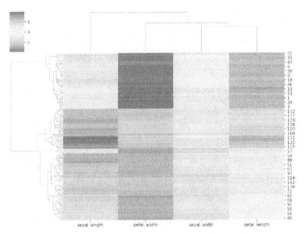

FIGURE 3.20: A cluster map created with Seaborn

SWARM PLOTS

The swarm plot positions each data point on the categorical axis with minimal overlap, giving a better representation of the distribution of values. In this section, we display a swarm plot for a built-in dataset in Seaborn.

Listing 3.21 displays the content of `swarm_plot.py` that ChatGPT generated to render contour lines using Seaborn.

LISTING 3.21: swarm_plot.py

```
import matplotlib.pyplot as plt
import seaborn as sns

def plot_swarm(data, x_col, y_col):
    sns.swarmplot(x=x_col, y=y_col, data=data)
    plt.show()

# Usage
data = sns.load_dataset("iris")
plot_swarm(data, "species", "sepal_length")
```

Listing 3.21 starts with two `import` statements and the `plot_swarm()` function that renders the swarm plot. The second part of Listing 3.21 initializes the Pandas DataFrame data with the contents of the Seaborn built-in dataset `iris`, and then invokes `plot_swarm()` with the variable `data`. Figure 3.21 shows the swarm plot that is rendered by launching the code in Listing 3.21.

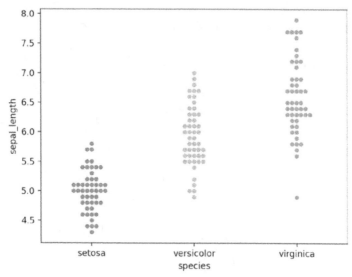

FIGURE 3.21: Swarm plot created with Seaborn

JOINT PLOTS FOR BIVARIATE DATA

Seaborn's `jointplot` displays a relationship between two variables. It combines scatter plots, regression plots, and even hexbin plots with histograms. Joint plots display a relationship between two variables along with their individual distributions.

Listing 3.22 displays the contents of `joint_plot.py` that ChatGPT generated to render a joint plot using Seaborn.

LISTING 3.22: joint_plot.py

```
import matplotlib.pyplot as plt
import seaborn as sns

def plot_jointplot(data, x_col, y_col, kind='scatter'):
    sns.jointplot(x=x_col, y=y_col, data=data, kind=kind)
    plt.show()

# Usage
data = sns.load_dataset("iris")
plot_jointplot(data, "sepal_length", "sepal_width", "hex")
```

Listing 3.22 starts with two `import` statements and the `plot_joint()` function that renders the joint plot. The second part of Listing 3.22 initializes the Pandas DataFrame data with the contents of the Seaborn built-in dataset iris, and then invokes `plot_pair()` with the variable `data`. Figure 3.22 shows the joint plot that is rendered by launching the code in Listing 3.22.

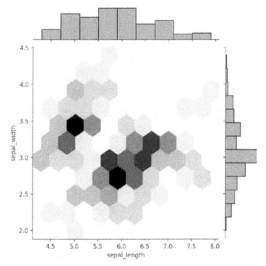

FIGURE 3.22: A joint plot created with Seaborn

POINT PLOTS FOR FACTORIZED VIEWS

Point plots can be useful to highlight the differences between points, especially when categorized by factors (like gender, as in the usage example). The lines connecting the points can help emphasize any trends as well as the comparison between points with lines.

Listing 3.23 displays the content of `point_plot.py` that ChatGPT generated to render a point plot using Seaborn.

LISTING 3.23: point_plot.py

```
import matplotlib.pyplot as plt
import seaborn as sns

def plot_pointplot(data, x_col, y_col, hue=None):
    sns.pointplot(x=x_col, y=y_col, hue=hue, data=data)
    plt.show()

# Usage
data = sns.load_dataset("tips")
plot_pointplot(data, "day", "total_bill", "sex")
```

Listing 3.23 starts with two `import` statements and the `plot_point-plot()` function that renders the point plot. The second part of Listing 3.23 initializes the Pandas DataFrame data with the contents of the Seaborn built-in dataset `tips`, and then invokes `plot_pointplot()` with the variable data. Figure 3.23 displays the point plot that is rendered by launching the code in Listing 3.23.

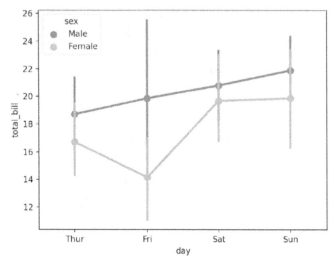

FIGURE 3.23: A point plot created with Seaborn

SEABORN'S KDE PLOTS FOR DENSITY ESTIMATIONS

Kernel Density Estimation (KDE) plots visualize the probability density of a continuous variable. They can be thought of as "smoothed histograms" and are particularly useful for discerning the underlying distribution of a dataset because they help us visualize the data density.

Listing 3.24 displays the content of `kde_plot.py` that ChatGPT generated to render a KDE plot using Seaborn.

LISTING 3.24: kde_plot.py

```
import matplotlib.pyplot as plt
import seaborn as sns

def plot_kde(data, column):
    sns.kdeplot(data[column], shade=True)
    plt.show()

# Usage
data = sns.load_dataset("iris")
plot_kde(data, "sepal_length")
```

Listing 3.24 starts with two `import` statements and the `plot_kde()` function that renders the KDE plot. The second part of Listing 3.23 initializes the Pandas DataFrame data with the contents of the Seaborn built-in dataset `iris`, and then invokes `plot_kde()` with the variable `data`. Figure 3.24 shows the point plot that is rendered by launching the code in Listing 3.24.

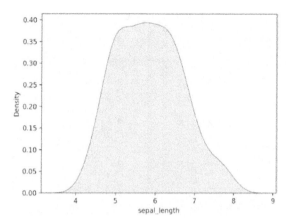

FIGURE 3.24: A KDE plot created with Seaborn

SEABORN'S RIDGE PLOTS

Ridge plots are essentially a series of KDE plots displayed on top of one another, allowing for the comparison of distributions across categories. As an illustration, Listing 3.25 displays the content of `ridge_plot.py` that ChatGPT generated to render a ridge plot using Seaborn.

LISTING 3.25: ridge_plot.py

```
import matplotlib.pyplot as plt
import seaborn as sns

def plot_ridge(data, x_col, category_col):
    g = sns.FacetGrid(data, row=category_col, hue=category_
col, aspect=5)
    g.map(sns.kdeplot, x_col, clip_on=False, shade=True,
alpha=1, lw=1.5, bw_method=0.2)
    g.map(sns.kdeplot, x_col, clip_on=False, color="w",
lw=1, bw_method=0.2)
    g.map(plt.axhline, y=0, lw=2, clip_on=False)
    plt.show()

# Usage
data = sns.load_dataset("diamonds")
subset_data = data[data['cut'].isin(['Ideal', 'Fair',
'Good'])]
plot_ridge(subset_data, "price", "cut")
```

Listing 3.25 starts with two `import` statements and the `plot_ridge()` function that renders the ridge plot. The second part of Listing 3.25 initializes the Pandas DataFrame data with the contents of the Seaborn built-in dataset `dia-monds`, and then invokes `plot_ridge()` with the variable `data`. Figure 3.25 shows the ridge plot that is rendered by launching the code in Listing 3.25.

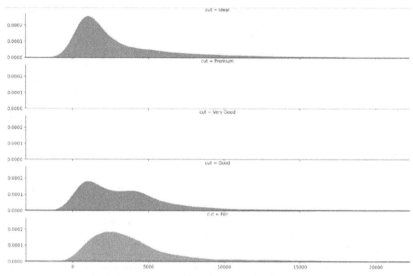

FIGURE 3.25: A ridge plot created with Seaborn

SUMMARY

This chapter contains Python-based solutions for a variety of tasks generated by ChatGPT. You learned about various types of charts and graphs and when to use them, along with the advantages and disadvantages of each type of chart and graph.

You learned about data visualization using a popular open-source Python-based library called Matplotlib that can render numerous types of charts and graphs.

You also learned how to render histograms, violin plots, and time series visualizations. By mastering these techniques, you can craft compelling narratives from data, aiding in decision-making and insight-generation. A well-crafted visualization is worth a thousand rows of raw data.

## CHAPTER 4

LINEAR REGRESSION WITH GPT-4

This chapter introduces linear regression and shows code samples of linear regression using NumPy APIs. The code samples use an "incremental" approach, starting with simple examples that involve Python and NumPy code (often using the NumPy `linspace()` API).

The first part of this chapter briefly discusses various types of linear regression, along with examples for simple linear regression, multiple linear regression, polynomial regression, and linear regression with interaction terms.

The second section of this chapter contains additional code samples involving linear regression tasks using standard techniques in NumPy. Hence, if you are comfortable with this topic, you can probably skim quickly through the first two sections of this chapter.

Before you read this chapter, keep in mind that most (around 90%) of the material was generated by ChatGPT. The editing process for the material in this chapter involved the following changes:

- the addition of section headings
- the inclusion of list item identifiers
- the removal of inconsequential details
- italicized headings

The purpose of the lists is to make it easier for you to read the material and adhere as much as possible to the layout of the material that ChatGPT has generated.

As you will soon see, the details in this chapter demonstrate the impressive ability of ChatGPT to provide fully detailed responses to tasks that are posed by users. In addition, ChatGPT has very helpful debugging capabilities that can assist in debugging the code that it generates for you because that code is not always perfect.

WHAT IS LINEAR REGRESSION?

Although linear regression was developed more than 200 years ago, this technique is still one of the core techniques for solving (albeit simple) problems in statistics and machine learning. In fact, the technique known as the Mean Squared Error (MSE) for finding a best fitting line for data points in a 2D plane (or a hyperplane for higher dimensions) is implemented in Python to minimize cost functions (which are discussed later).

The goal of linear regression is to find the best fitting line that "represents" a dataset. Keep in mind two important points. First, the best fitting line does not necessarily pass through all (or even most of) the points in the dataset. The purpose of a best fitting line is to minimize the vertical distance of that line from the points in the dataset. Second, linear regression does not determine the best fitting polynomial: the latter involves finding a higher-degree polynomial that passes through many of the points in a dataset.

EXAMPLES OF LINEAR REGRESSION

Linear regression is a statistical method used to model the relationship between a dependent variable and one or more independent variables. The simplest form of linear regression, simple linear regression, involves one dependent variable and one independent variable. By contrast, multiple linear regression involves one dependent variable and two or more independent variables. The following are some examples of types of regression:

- simple linear regression
- multiple linear regression
- polynomial regression
- linear regression with interaction terms

The choice of the type of linear regression to use depends on the nature of the data and the specific questions you are trying to answer. For instance, an example of simple linear regression involves predicting a person's weight based on their height. Suppose that you have data on the heights and weights of a group of people. You want to predict weight (dependent variable) based on height (independent variable). The mathematical representation of weight and height is as follows:

```
Weight=β0+β1×Height
```

An example of multiple linear regression involves predicting the price of a house based on its size and age. In this case, you are predicting the house price (dependent variable) based on two independent variables: the size of the house (in square feet) and age of the house (in years). The mathematical representation for price, size, and age is as follows:

```
Price=β0+β1×Size+β2×Age
```

A third example involves linear regression with interaction terms, such as predicting the sales of a product based on its price and the amount of advertising, while also considering the interaction between price and advertising.

Besides the direct effect of price and advertising on sales, you must also consider how the combination of the two (their interaction) might influence sales. The mathematical representation for sales, price, advertising, and the product of price and advertising is as follows:

```
Sales=β0+β1×Price+β2×Advertising+β3×(Price×Advertising)
```

In addition to the preceding examples, it is possible to perform polynomial regression (a type of linear regression), such as predicting the trajectory of a projectile based on time. Even though it is called "polynomial," it is still a form of linear regression because the regression coefficients (betas) are linear. The non-linearity is in the independent variable. The mathematical representation (for a second-degree polynomial) for this example is as follows:

```
Height=β0+β1×Time+β2×Time2
```

Yet another example involves linear regression with categorical predictors involves predicting a person's salary based on their education level (e.g., high school, bachelor's, or master's). This involves using dummy variables to represent the categorical predictors. The mathematical representation (assuming "high school" is the reference category) is as follows:

```
Salary=β0+β1×Bachelor's+β2×Master's
```

The coefficients for the dummy variables (i.e., $\beta 1$ and $\beta 2$) represent the difference in the mean salary relative to the reference category.

METRICS FOR LINEAR REGRESSION

Evaluating the performance of a linear regression model is crucial in understanding how well the model fits the data and in comparing it with other models.

No single metric can provide a complete picture of the model's performance. It is essential to consider multiple metrics and understand the context of the problem you are addressing.

Here are some common metrics used to evaluate linear regression models:

- Coefficient of Determination (R^2, shown in the code as R^2)
- MSE
- Root Mean Squared Error (RMSE)
- Mean Absolute Error (MAE)

- Residual Standard Error (RSE)
- F-statistic
- Adjusted R^2
- Akaike Information Criterion (AIC)
- Durbin-Watson Statistic
- Variance Inflation Factor (VIF)

The following subsections contain brief descriptions of the topics in the preceding list.

Coefficient of Determination (R^2)

R^2 ("R squared," shown as `R^2` in the code) represents the proportion of the variance for the dependent variable that is explained by the independent variable(s) in the regression model. Its value ranges from 0 to 1, with 1 indicating that the model explains all the variability of the response data around its mean. Here is the formula:

```
R^2=1-(Residual Sum of Squares (RSS))/(Total Sum of Squares (TSS))
```

The MSE represents the average of the squares of the errors or deviations (i.e., difference between estimator and what is estimated). Here is the formula:

```
MSE = (∑(yi-y^i)^2)/n
```

In the preceding formula, `yi` is the actual value, `y^i` is the predicted value, and `n` is the number of observations.

The RMSE represents the square root of the MSE. It provides the magnitude of error in the same units as the original data.

The MAE represents the average absolute differences between the observed actual outcomes and the forecasts. The formula is as follows:

```
MAE = (∑|yi-y^i|)/n
```

The RSE represents the standard deviation of the residuals. It gives a measure of how spread out the residuals are around the line of best fit. Here is the formula:

```
RSE = sqrt((∑(yi-y^i)^2)/df)
```

In the preceding formula, `yi` is the observed value, `y` is the predicted value, and `df` is the degrees of freedom (the total number of observations). Smaller values for the RSE are indicative of a better fitting model because the data points will be more closely "packed" around the regression line.

The F-statistic is used in the context of an ANOVA (analysis of variance) test that provides a statistical test of whether there is a significant relationship between the dependent variable and the independent variables. It compares the full model against a model with no predictors.

The t-statistic involves testing whether a given coefficient is different from 0 (no effect). A large t-statistic (or one that is far from zero) and a small p-value suggest that the coefficient is statistically significant.

The adjusted R^2 is adjusted for the number of predictors in the model. Unlike R^2, it penalizes the addition of extraneous predictors, and it is useful when comparing models with a different number of predictors.

The AIC and BIC (Bayesian Information Criterion) are used for model selection. They balance the goodness of fit of the model against the complexity of the model. The model with the lowest AIC or BIC is preferred.

The Durbin-Watson Statistic involves tests for autocorrelation in the residuals, and it is useful in time series data.

The VIF measures how much the variance of an estimated regression coefficient increases when your predictors are correlated. If no factors are correlated, the VIFs will be equal to 1.

LINEAR REGRESSION WITH RANDOM DATA WITH GPT-4

Listing 4.1 displays the content of `linreg_gpt4.py` that illustrates how to use the NumPy `randn()` API to generate a dataset and then the `scatter()` API in Matplotlib to plot the points in the dataset.

NOTE *The description of the code in Listing 4.1 was prepared by the author and not by ChatGPT.*

LISTING 4.1: linreg_gpt4.py

```
"""
A simple linear regression example using Python's scikit-
learn library.
1. Generate Sample Data
First, let's generate some synthetic data. Suppose we
are trying to model the relationship between years of
experience and salary.
"""

import numpy as np
import matplotlib.pyplot as plt

# Generate synthetic data
np.random.seed(0)  # for reproducibility

# Random years of experience between 0 to 2.5 years
X = 2.5 * np.random.rand(100, 1)

# Salary = base + 3*Experience + noise
y = 5 + 3 * X + np.random.randn(100, 1)

plt.scatter(X, y)
```

```
plt.xlabel("Years of Experience")
plt.ylabel("Salary")
plt.title("Experience vs. Salary")
plt.show()
"""

In the above code:
X represents years of experience.
y represents the corresponding salary.
We assume a base salary of 5, and for each year of
experience, the salary increases by 3 units. In addition,
there's some random noise.
"""


"""
2. Train a Linear Regression Model
let's fit a linear regression model to this data.
"""

from sklearn.linear_model import LinearRegression

# Create a linear regression model
reg = LinearRegression()

# Fit the model to the data
reg.fit(X, y)

# Get the regression coefficients
intercept = reg.intercept_[0]
slope = reg.coef_[0][0]

print(f"Intercept (base salary): {intercept:.2f}")
print(f"Slope (salary increase per year of experience):
{slope:.2f}")
"""

In the code above:
Use LinearRegression() from scikit-learn for a linear
regression model.
The fit method trains the model using our synthetic data.
The intercept_ gives the base salary (y-intercept), and
coef_ provides the increase in salary for each additional
year of experience (slope).


3. Visualize the Regression Line
Let's plot the data points and the regression line.
"""
# Predict values
y_pred = reg.predict(X)
```

```
plt.scatter(X, y)
plt.plot(X, y_pred, color='red')
plt.xlabel("Years of Experience")
plt.ylabel("Salary")
plt.title("Experience vs. Salary with Regression Line")
plt.show()
"""
```

In the visualization, data points are shown as blue dots.
The red line is the linear regression model's prediction.

4. Evaluate the Model
Finally, let's compute the RMSE to evaluate the performance
of our model.
"""

```
from sklearn.metrics import mean_squared_error
rmse = np.sqrt(mean_squared_error(y, y_pred))
print(f"Root Mean Squared Error: {rmse:.2f}")
```


"""
In this step:
Use the mean_squared_error function in scikit-learn to
compute the MSE.
The square root of the MSE gives us the RMSE, which
indicates the model's prediction error in the same units as
the target variable.
This entire process allows us to understand the
relationship between experience and salary, model it using
linear regression, and evaluate the performance of the
model.
"""

Listing 4.1 starts with two import statements, followed by formulas for X and y that generate quasi-random value for y based on the values in X. Next, a scatter plot is displayed based on the values for X and y.

The next portion of Listing 4.1 initializes the variable reg as an instance of the class LinearRegression, and then invokes the fit() method to fit the model to the data in the CSV file death.csv. Now we can initialize the variable intercept and slope from the fitted model with this pair of code snippets:

```
intercept = reg.intercept_[0]
slope = reg.coef_[0][0]
```

Launch the code in Listing 4.1, and you will see two graphs displayed. Figure 4.1 shows the data points, and Figure 4.2 displays the data point with the best fitting line.

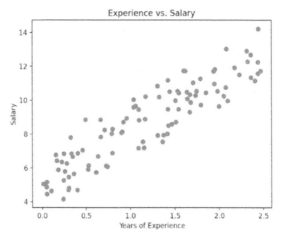

FIGURE 4.1 The set of data points

FIGURE 4.2 The best fitting line

LINEAR REGRESSION WITH A DATASET WITH GPT-4

The example in this section uses linear regression on the `death.csv` dataset that was downloaded from the following website:

https://data.world/nrippner/cancer-linear-regression-model-tutorial

For your convenience, Listing 4.2 displays a portion of the contents of the CSV file `death.csv`.

LISTING 4.2: *death.csv*

```
county,fips,met_objective_of_45_5_1,age_adjusted_death_
rate,lower_95_confidence_interval_for_death_rate,upper_95_
confidence_interval_for_death_rate,average_deaths_per_
year,recent_trend_2,recent_5_year_trend_2_in_death_
```

```
rates,lower_95_confidence_interval_for_trend,upper_95_
confidence_interval_for_trend
United States,0,No,46,45.9,46.1,"157,376",falli
ng,-2.4,-2.6,-2.2
"Perry County, Kentucky",21193,No,125.6,108.9,144.2,43,stab
le,-0.6,-2.7,1.6
"Powell County, Kentucky",21197,No,125.3,100.2,155.1,18,sta
ble,1.7,0,3.4
"North Slope Borough, Alaska",2185,
No,124.9,73,194.7,5,**,**,**,**
// details omitted for brevity
"Yakutat City and Borough, Alaska<sup>3</sup>",2282,*,*,*,*
,*,**,**,**,**
"Yukon-Koyukuk Census Area,
Alaska",2290,*,*,*,*,*,**,**,**,**
"Zapata County, Texas",48505,*,*,*,*,*,*,*,*,*
"Zavala County, Texas",48507,*,*,*,*,*,**,**,**,**
"Ziebach County, South Dakota",46137,*,*,*,*,*,**,**,**,**
```

Let's perform linear regression on this dataset using GPT-4, starting with the upload of the `death.csv` dataset. You can perform this step in ChatGPT by selecting "GPT-4" and then click on the "+" symbol at the bottom of the screen, after which you upload the dataset from your laptop.

At this point, we are ready to perform a sequence of steps to analyze and prepare the `death.csv` dataset for linear regression:

1. Describe the features of the `death.csv` dataset.
2. Describe the preparation process of the `death.csv` dataset.
3. Describe the exploratory analysis.
4. Describe the model selection.
5. Describe the model diagnostics.

Each of the steps in the preceding list is discussed in the following subsections. Some of the subsections are quite lengthy, so it might be more efficient for you to skim the sections and then return for an in-depth reading of these subsections.

DESCRIBE THE FEATURES OF THE DEATH.CSV DATASET

Based on the contents of the provided dataset, here is a detailed description of the features (shown in italics):

- *county:*
    a. Description: The name of the county or region
    b. Type: Categorical (Nominal)
    c. Example Values: "United States," "Perry County, Kentucky", and "Powell County, Kentucky"
    d. Usage: Can be used as an identifier for each data point

- *fips:*
  a. Description: Federal Information Processing Standards (FIPS) code, a unique identifier for each county in the US
  b. Type: Numeric (although used as a categorical identifier)
  c. Example Values: 0 (for the United States as a whole), 21193, and 21197
  d. Usage: Can be used as a unique identifier, especially for joining with other datasets that use FIPS codes
- *met_objective_of_45_5_1:*
  a. Description: Indicates whether a specific objective (possibly a target death rate of 45.5) was met
  b. Type: Categorical (Binary)
  c. Example Values: "Yes" and "No"
  d. Usage: Can be used to evaluate and compare the performance of different counties against a set standard or objective
- *age_adjusted_death_rate:*
  a. Description: The death rate adjusted for age to allow for comparison between regions with different age distributions
  b. Type: Numeric
  c. Example Values: 46, 125.6, and 125.3
  d. Usage: A key metric for understanding the overall death rate, independent of the age distribution
- *lower_95_confidence_interval_for_death_rate & upper_95_confidence_interval_for_death_rate:*
  a. Description: Lower and upper bounds of the 95% confidence interval for the age-adjusted death rate. Gives an idea of the uncertainty or variability around the estimated death rate.
  b. Type: Numeric
  c. Example Values: For lower: 45.9, 108.9, and 100.2. For upper: 46.1, 144.2, and 155.1.
  d. Usage: Helps in understanding the reliability and range of the estimated death rates
- *average_deaths_per_year:*
  a. Description: The average number of deaths occurring per year
  b. Type: Numeric
  c. Example Values: 157, 376, 43, and 18
  d. Usage: Gives an absolute measure of the number of deaths, which can be used for further analysis or planning
- *recent_trend_2:*
  a. Description: Indicates the recent trend in deaths
  b. Type: Categorical (Ordinal)
  c. Example Values: "falling," "stable," and "**" (likely representing missing or undefined data)
  d. Usage: Provides insight into whether the death rate is increasing, decreasing, or remaining stable over a recent period

- *recent_5_year_trend_2_in_death_rates:*
  a. Description: The change in death rates over a recent 5-year period
  b. Type: Numeric
  c. Example Values: −2.4, −0.6, and 1.7
  d. Usage: Indicates the rate of change in death rates, which can be useful for forecasting or understanding recent patterns
- *lower_95_confidence_interval_for_trend & upper_95_confidence_interval_for_trend:*
  a. Description: Lower and upper bounds of the 95% confidence interval for the recent 5-year trend in death rates
  b. Type: Numeric
  c. Example Values: For lower: −2.6, −2.7, and 0. For upper: −2.2, 1.6, and 3.4.
  d. Usage: Provides a range of estimates for the trend, offering insight into its reliability and variability

These features provide both absolute and relative metrics related to death rates in different counties, allowing for comprehensive analysis, comparison, and understanding of patterns and trends over time.

THE PREPARATION PROCESS OF THE DATASET

To describe the preparation process of the `death.csv` dataset, we begin by inspecting the contents of the dataset. We check its structure, the first few rows, and the overall statistics. This will give us an idea of what we are working with and what kind of preparation might have been involved.

Let's start by loading and inspecting the dataset, which has the following structure:

- Rows: 3141 entries (including one for the United States as a whole)
- Columns: 11 columns

The description of each column is as follows:

- *county:* The name of the county (or "United States" for the national average)
- *fips:* Federal Information Processing Standards (FIPS) code for the county
- *met_objective_of_45_5_1:* Indicates whether a certain objective was met (values appear to be "Yes" or "No")
- *age_adjusted_death_rate:* The death rate adjusted for age
- *lower_95_confidence_interval_for_death_rate:* Lower bound of the 95% confidence interval for the death rate
- *upper_95_confidence_interval_for_death_rate:* Upper bound of the 95% confidence interval for the death rate

- *average_deaths_per_year:* Average number of deaths per year
- *recent_trend_2:* Recent trend in deaths
- *recent_5_year_trend_2_in_death_rates:* 5-year trend in death rates
- *lower_95_confidence_interval_for_trend:* Lower bound of the 95% confidence interval for the trend
- *upper_95_confidence_interval_for_trend:* Upper bound of the 95% confidence interval for the trend

Observations:

Most columns are of the object data type, which suggests that there might be non-numeric values or missing values denoted with special characters (like "**" in the *recent_trend_2* and *recent_5_year_trend_2_in_death_rates* columns). Some numeric values, like in the *average_deaths_per_year* column, are represented with commas, which is why they are treated as an object data type.

Preparation Process:

Based on the dataset structure and the observations, here is a probable preparation process for the death.csv dataset:

1. *Data Collection:*
2. The data was likely collected from various county-level and national databases or health organizations.
3. *Data Cleaning:*
4. Handling missing values. Special characters like "**" could be used to denote missing or unavailable data.
5. *Formatting:* Numbers might have been formatted to include commas for readability.
6. *Feature Engineering:*
   a. Calculation of confidence intervals: The 95% confidence intervals for death rates and trends suggest statistical calculations were performed post data collection.
   b. Age adjustment: The death rate has been adjusted for age, indicating some form of standardization.
7. *Data Transformation:* Data could have been transformed or aggregated to represent averages, trends, and other metrics at the county level.
8. *Data Annotation:* Columns like *met_objective_of_45_5_1* suggest that certain metrics or objectives were evaluated and annotated in the dataset.
9. *Data Validation:* Ensured the FIPS code matched with the correct county, and there are no duplicates or inconsistencies in the dataset.

To further understand and suggest improvements, we can conduct more in-depth exploratory data analysis (EDA) and quality checks, which are shown in the next section.

THE EXPLORATORY ANALYSIS

EDA is an approach to analyzing datasets, often prior to formal modeling or hypothesis testing. The main goal of EDA is to understand the data, its structure, outliers, and patterns, and to identify potential anomalies or peculiarities. Here is a structured description of the EDA process for the `death.csv` dataset:

1. *Univariate Analysis:*
   a. Analyze one variable at a time.
   b. For numeric variables, describe the central tendency (mean, median) and dispersion (range, variance, standard deviation). Histograms, box plots, and density plots can be useful.
   c. For categorical variables, use bar plots to understand the frequency or proportion of each category.
2. *Bivariate Analysis:*
   a. Analyze the relationship between two variables.
   b. Use scatter plots for continuous-continuous pairs.
   c. Use box plots for categorical-continuous pairs.
   d. Use stacked column charts or mosaic plots for categorical-categorical pairs.
3. *Multivariate Analysis:*
   a. Analyze more than two variables simultaneously.
   b. Use correlation matrices or heatmaps to understand relationships between continuous variables.
   c. Use pair plots or 3D scatter plots for a visual representation of relationships.
4. *Checking for Missing Values:*
   a. Identify columns with missing values.
   b. Analyze patterns of missingness. Are they missing at random or is there a pattern?
5. *Outlier Detection:*
   a. Detect unusual or suspicious values.
   b. Use visual methods (box plots, scatter plots) or statistical methods (IQR, Z-scores).
6. *Feature Engineering:*
   a. Create new variables from existing ones.
   b. For example, from the dataset, one could derive a feature indicating if a county's death rate is above or below the national average.
7. *Data Quality Checks:*
   a. Ensure that data is consistent, accurate, and reliable.
   b. For instance, FIPS codes should be unique to each county.

8. *Correlation Analysis:*
   a. Understand how different continuous variables move in relation to each other.
   b. Use the Pearson correlation for continuous variables and Cramér's V for categorical variables.

9. *Trend Analysis:*
   a. Especially relevant for the *recent_5_year_trend_2_in_death_rates* feature in our dataset.
   b. Understand upward or downward trends in data over time.

10. *Distribution Analysis:*
    a. Examine the distribution of key metrics (e.g., *age_adjusted_death_rate*).
    b. Check for normality, skewness, and kurtosis.

11. *Geospatial Analysis:*
    a. Since the dataset contains county information, it would be possible (with additional geographic data) to visualize metrics on a map, highlighting regions of interest.

12. *Summary Reports:*
    a. Summarize findings, perhaps in the form of a dashboard or a report, highlighting key insights from the data.

13. *Hypothesis Generation:*
    a. Based on the findings, generate hypotheses to be tested in subsequent analyses or modeling. After EDA, the analyst should have a deeper understanding of the dataset's characteristics and its potential limitations. It provides insights that can guide the subsequent modeling process and ensures that the assumptions made during modeling are valid.

DETAILED EDA ON THE DEATH.CSV DATASET

Let's conduct a detailed EDA on the death.csv dataset. The steps are

- Univariate Analysis - To understand individual features
- Bivariate Analysis - To understand the relationships between pairs of features
- Missing Values Analysis - To identify and understand any missing data
- Outlier Detection - To identify potential outliers in the dataset
- Distribution Analysis - To understand the distribution of key metrics

Let's begin with the univariate analysis for a deeper understanding of individual features:

- *age_adjusted_death_rate:*
  Most counties have an age-adjusted death rate between 20 and 60. There are few counties with very high death rates, which could be considered outliers.

- *lower_95_confidence_interval_for_death_rate & upper_95_confidence_interval_for_death_rate:*
  The distributions of the lower and upper 95% confidence intervals for death rate are similar to the distribution of the age-adjusted death rate. This is expected since they provide a range of estimates around the death rate.
- *recent_5_year_trend_2_in_death_rates:*
  The 5-year trend in death rates seems to be centered around zero, suggesting that for many counties, the death rates have remained stable. There are counties with both increasing and decreasing trends.
- *lower_95_confidence_interval_for_trend & upper_95_confidence_interval_for_trend:*
  These distributions represent the range of estimates for the 5-year trend in death rates. They provide context for the variability and reliability of the trend estimates.

Next, let's examine the categorical features and understand their distributions from their univariate analysis:

- *met_objective_of_45_5_1:*
  A significant number of counties have not met the objective (indicated by "No"), while a smaller portion have met the objective (indicated by "Yes").
- *recent_trend_2:*
  The majority of counties have a "stable" recent trend in deaths. A considerable number of counties have a "falling" trend. Fewer counties have a "rising" trend in deaths. Some entries are marked with "**," which likely indicates missing or undefined data.

Let's move on to the bivariate analysis to explore relationships between pairs of features. We will start by analyzing the correlation between the numeric features using a heatmap:

- *age_adjusted_death_rate* is highly correlated with both *lower_95_confidence_interval_for_death_rate* and *upper_95_confidence_interval_for_death_rate*. This is expected, as the confidence intervals provide the range of uncertainty around the death rate.
- Similarly, *recent_5_year_trend_2_in_death_rates* have a high correlation with *lower_95_confidence_interval_for_trend* and *upper_95_confidence_interval_for_trend*.
- The correlations among other pairs of variables are relatively low.

Next, let's analyze the missing values in the dataset to understand if there is any missing data and decide how to handle it. The missing values analysis reveals the following information:

- *recent_5_year_trend_2_in_death_rates, lower_95_confidence_interval_for_trend, and upper_95_confidence_interval_for_trend:*
  All have the same count of missing values, which is 447 (or about 14.23% of the data). This suggests that when the trend data is missing, its corresponding confidence intervals are also missing.
- *age_adjusted_death_rate, lower_95_confidence_interval_for_death_rate, and upper_95_confidence_interval_for_death_rate:*
  All have the same count of missing values, which is 328 (or about 10.44% of the data). Similar to the trend columns, when the death rate data is missing, its corresponding confidence intervals are also missing.

Next, let's move on to outlier detection. We will use box plots to visually identify potential outliers in the numeric columns:

- *age_adjusted_death_rate:*
  There are a few data points above the upper whisker that can be considered as potential outliers. These represent counties with exceptionally high age-adjusted death rates.
- *lower_95_confidence_interval_for_death_rate & upper_95_confidence_interval_for_death_rate:*
  Both of these features show potential outliers above their respective upper whiskers, consistent with the outliers in the age-adjusted death rate.
- *recent_5_year_trend_2_in_death_rates:*
  There are data points both above and below the whiskers, indicating counties with unusually high or low trends in death rates over the recent 5 years.
- *lower_95_confidence_interval_for_trend & upper_95_confidence_interval_for_trend:*
  Both of these features exhibit potential outliers, consistent with the outliers in the recent 5-year trend.

Next, let's analyze the distribution of some key metrics, focusing on their skewness and kurtosis. Skewness provides insights into the symmetry of the distribution, while kurtosis reveals information about its "tailedness."

- *age_adjusted_death_rate:*
  a. Skewness (0.55): The distribution is moderately right skewed, meaning there is a tail on the right side. This indicates that there are some counties with exceptionally high death rates.
  b. Kurtosis (1.29): This value suggests a distribution with heavier tails than a normal distribution, indicating the presence of outliers.
- *lower_95_confidence_interval_for_death_rate & upper_95_confidence_interval_for_death_rate:*
  Both have skewness values indicating a right-skewed distribution, with the upper confidence interval being more skewed. Their kurtosis values suggest heavier tails than a normal distribution.

- *recent_5_year_trend_2_in_death_rates:*
  a. Skewness (−2.35): The distribution is significantly left-skewed, meaning there is a tail on the left side. This indicates that many counties have a decreasing trend in death rates.
  b. Kurtosis (58.03): This high value indicates the presence of extreme outliers or sharp peaks in the distribution.
- *lower_95_confidence_interval_for_trend & upper_95_confidence_interval_for_trend:*
  Both these features exhibit high skewness and kurtosis values, indicating non-normal distributions with pronounced tails and potential outliers.

These insights from the distribution analysis can guide further statistical analysis, hypothesis testing, and modeling efforts. For the next steps in EDA, we delve deeper into bivariate and multivariate analyses to understand the relationships between features.

BIVARIATE AND MULTIVARIATE ANALYSES

Let's explore the relationships between features using bivariate and multivariate analyses:

Bivariate Analysis:
- Scatter plots between continuous variables to visualize relationships.
- Box plots for categorical-continuous pairs to see how a continuous variable varies across different categories.
- Crosstabs or stacked bar plots for categorical-categorical pairs to understand the distribution of categories across different groups.

Multivariate Analysis:
- Pair plots to view relationships between multiple continuous variables simultaneously
- Correlation heatmaps to understand linear relationships between continuous variables

Let's start with the bivariate analysis:
We will create scatter plots using the *age_adjusted_death_rate* and other continuous features to understand their relationships.
The scatter plots provide insights into the relationship between *age_adjusted_death_rate* and other continuous features:

- *age_adjusted_death_rate vs. lower_95_confidence_interval_for_death_rate & age_adjusted_death_rate vs. upper_95_confidence_interval_for_death_rate:*
  These plots exhibit a strong linear relationship, which is expected since the confidence intervals provide bounds around the age-adjusted death rate.

- *age_adjusted_death_rate vs. recent_5_year_trend_2_in_death_rates:*
The relationship here does not seem to be linear. While many counties have a stable trend around zero, there is a spread of data points across different death rates, indicating that the overall death rate is not necessarily predictive of the recent trend.
- *age_adjusted_death_rate vs. lower_95_confidence_interval_for_trend &*
age_adjusted_death_rate vs. upper_95_confidence_interval_for_trend:
These plots show a dispersed pattern, suggesting that the confidence intervals for the trend do not have a straightforward linear relationship with the age-adjusted death rate.

Next, let's analyze the relationship between the categorical feature *recent_trend_2* and the continuous feature *age_adjusted_death_rate* using a box plot. This will help us understand how the age-adjusted death rate varies across different recent trends (rising, falling, stable). The box plot illustrates the distribution of the *age_adjusted_death_rate* across different recent trends:

- *Falling:*
Counties with a falling trend tend to have higher median death rates, but there is a widespread, suggesting variability in the extent of the decrease among these counties.
- *Stable:*
Counties with a stable trend have a lower median death rate compared to those with a falling trend. The interquartile range (IQR) is also narrower, indicating less variability among these counties.
- *Rising:*
Counties with a rising trend in death rates show a lower median compared to those with a falling trend but higher than those with a stable trend. The distribution appears more compact with fewer outliers.
- *'** (undefined or missing data):*
This category seems to have a similar distribution to the stable trend, but it is important to investigate and understand the meaning or reason for these undefined entries.

Next, for the multivariate analysis, let's create a pair plot for a subset of continuous features to visualize pairwise relationships and distributions. We will focus on *age_adjusted_death_rate, recent_5_year_trend_2_in_death_rates,* and their respective confidence intervals.
The pair plot provides an overview of pairwise relationships and individual distributions for the selected features:

- *Diagonal KDE Plots:*
These plots show the distribution of individual features.
As observed earlier, *age_adjusted_death_rate* is moderately right-skewed, while the *recent_5_year_trend_2_in_death_rates* are left-skewed.

- *Off-Diagonal Scatter Plots:*
  The scatter plots between *age_adjusted_death_rate* and its confidence intervals (both lower and upper) show strong linear relationships, as expected.

The relationship between *age_adjusted_death_rate* and *recent_5_year_trend_2_in_death_rates* does not exhibit a clear trend, confirming our earlier observation.

Now, to further explore the multivariate relationships, let's create a correlation heatmap using a wider set of continuous features. This will give us insight into linear relationships between these features.

The extended correlation heatmap reinforces some of our earlier observations and provides additional insights:

- *age_adjusted_death_rate and its confidence intervals:*
  As seen before, there is a high correlation between the *age_adjusted_death_rate* and its lower and upper 95% confidence intervals. This is expected, as these intervals provide bounds around the primary metric.
- *recent_5_year_trend_2_in_death_rates and its confidence intervals:*
  Similarly, the *recent_5_year_trend_2_in_death_rates* also exhibit a high correlation with its respective confidence intervals.
- *age_adjusted_death_rate and recent_5_year_trend_2_in_death_rates:*
  The correlation between these two is relatively low, suggesting that the overall death rate is not strongly linearly related to the recent 5-year trend in death rates.
- *Confidence Intervals:*
  The confidence intervals for the death rate and the trend are correlated with each other to some extent, which makes sense since they are derived from the same underlying data.

We have now completed a comprehensive EDA on the `death.csv` dataset. We investigated individual features, analyzed bivariate relationships, and explored multivariate associations. The insights gained from this EDA can inform subsequent modeling, hypothesis testing, and further analyses.

THE MODEL SELECTION PROCESS

The model selection process involves choosing the best machine learning or statistical model for a particular dataset and problem. This process is crucial because the success of your predictions or inferences largely depends on the model you choose. Here is a structured description of the model selection process:

1. *Define the Problem:*
   a. Clearly define the objective: Is it a classification, regression, clustering, or another type of problem?
   b. Determine the evaluation metric: For instance, accuracy might be suitable for balanced classification problems, but precision, recall, or the

F1-score might be more appropriate for imbalanced datasets. For regression problems, you might consider metrics like the RMSE or MAE.

2. *Baseline Model:*

Start with a simple model to serve as a benchmark. This could be a linear regression for regression problems or a logistic regression for classification tasks. The idea is to have a basic measure of performance to which you can compare more complex models.

3. *Choose Candidate Models:*

Based on the problem type and data characteristics, shortlist a set of algorithms that are known to work well for such problems. For example, for structured tabular data, algorithms like decision trees, random forest, gradient boosting machines, and SVMs might be considered. For unstructured data like images, you might consider deep learning models.

4. *Data Preparation:*

Different algorithms might require different data preprocessing steps. Normalize or standardize data for algorithms like SVM or neural networks. Handle categorical variables using encoding techniques like one-hot encoding, especially for algorithms that do not handle categorical data natively. Ensure the data is split into training and validation (and possibly test) sets.

5. *Hyperparameter Tuning:*

Almost every algorithm has hyperparameters that need to be set. These can greatly influence performance. Use techniques like grid search, random search, or Bayesian optimization to find the optimal hyperparameters for each candidate model.

6. *Cross-Validation:*

To ensure that your model's performance is robust and not overly optimistic, use cross-validation. K-fold cross-validation is a common technique. Cross-validation provides a more generalized performance metric for the model on unseen data.

7. *Model Evaluation:*

Evaluate each model using your chosen metric(s) on the validation set. Compare the performance of different models against the baseline and against each other.

8. *Ensembling:*

If individual models are not performing well enough, consider combining multiple models. Techniques like bagging, boosting, or stacking can often result in better performance than individual models.

9. *Model Interpretability*

It is not always about getting the highest accuracy; sometimes understanding why a model makes certain decisions is crucial. Depending on the domain (like healthcare or finance), you might prioritize simpler, more interpretable models over black-box models, even if the latter has slightly better performance.

10. *Final Model Selection:*

    Based on validation performance, interpretability, and business objectives, select the final model. Train this model on the combined training and validation set to make final predictions on the test set.

11. *Deployment and Monitoring:*

    Once the final model is selected and evaluated, it can be deployed in a production environment. Continuously monitor the model's performance in the real world. Over time, as data evolves, the model might need retraining or fine-tuning.

12. *Feedback Loop:*

    As the model is used and predictions are collected, this data can be fed back into the training dataset for future model improvements.

The goal of the model selection process is not always to find the model with the highest performance metric. It is to find a model that meets the business objectives, is reliable, interpretable (if needed), and generalizes well to unseen data.

CODE FOR LINEAR REGRESSION WITH THE DEATH.CSV DATASET

Let's implement linear regression using the `death.csv` dataset. Here is a step-by-step process we will follow:

1. Data Preprocessing: Handle missing values and prepare the data for modeling.
2. Feature Selection: Choose the independent variables (features) that we'll use to predict the dependent variable.
3. Data Splitting: Split the dataset into training and testing sets.
4. Model Training: Train a linear regression model on the training set.
5. Model Evaluation: Evaluate the model's performance on the test set.
6. Model Interpretation: Interpret the model's coefficients.

For this demonstration, let's use the *age_adjusted_death_rate* as the dependent variable and *recent_5_year_trend_2_in_death_rates* as the independent variable.

Let's begin with data preprocessing. The linear regression model's performance on the test data is as follows:

- MSE: 145.22145.22
- R squared (R^2 or R^2) Value: 0.11140.1114

The R^2 value suggests that about 11.14% of the variance in the *age_adjusted_death_rate* is explained by the *recent_5_year_trend_2_in_death_rates*. This is not a very high value, indicating that the linear model using just the recent 5-year trend might not be sufficient to capture all the variability in the death rates.

Finally, let's proceed to model interpretation by examining the model's coefficients.

The linear regression model can be represented by the following equation:

```
age_adjusted_death_rate = 1.5506*recent_5_year_trend_2_in_
death_rates + 54.9239
```

Interpreting the coefficients:
The coefficient of `recent_5_year_trend_2_in_death_rates` equal 1.5506. For every unit increase in the *recent_5_year_trend_2_in_death_rates*, the *age_adjusted_death_rate* increases by approximately 1.5506 units, keeping all other factors constant. When the *recent_5_year_trend_2_in_death_rates* is zero, the predicted age_adjusted_death_rate is approximately 54.9239 (the intercept).

Given the moderate R^2 value, it is essential to consider other features or even more advanced modeling techniques to improve the predictive power, if needed. This linear model provides a basic understanding and relationship between the two variables.

Listing 4.3 displays the content of `linreg2_gpt4.py` that illustrates how to perform linear regression using a subset of the rows in the `death.csv` dataset.

LISTING 4.3: linreg2_gpt4.py

```
import pandas as pd
from sklearn.linear_model import LinearRegression
from sklearn.model_selection import train_test_split
from sklearn.metrics import mean_squared_error, r2_score

# the CSV death_clean.csv is described later:
death_df = pd.read_csv('death_clean.csv')

# Step 1: Data Preprocessing
# Drop rows with missing values in the columns of interest
processed_data = death_df.dropna(subset=["age_adjusted_
death_rate", "recent_5_year_trend_2_in_death_rates"])

# Step 2: Feature Selection
X = processed_data[["recent_5_year_trend_2_in_death_
rates"]]   # Independent variable
y = processed_data["age_adjusted_death_rate"]   # Dependent
variable

# Step 3: Data Splitting
X_train, X_test, y_train, y_test = train_test_split(X, y,
test_size=0.2, random_state=42)

# Step 4: Model Training
linear_reg = LinearRegression()
linear_reg.fit(X_train, y_train)
```

```
# Step 5: Model Evaluation
y_pred = linear_reg.predict(X_test)
mse = mean_squared_error(y_test, y_pred)
r2 = r2_score(y_test, y_pred)

# this code snippet added by the author:
print("mse:",mse,"r2:",r2)
```

Listing 4.3 starts with several import statements, followed by initializing the Pandas data frame `death_df` with the contents of the CSV file `death_clean.csv`. Note that this CSV file was created by the author by removing the data points in `death_clean.csv` that contain one or more asterisks.

The next portion of Listing 4.3 initializes the Pandas data frame `processed_data` that consists of dropping two columns in the data frame `death_df` with this code snippet:

```
processed_data = death_df.dropna(subset=["age_adjusted_
death_rate", "recent_5_year_trend_2_in_death_rates"])
```

Now that we have a validated dataset, we can initialize the independent variable X and the dependent variable y with this pair of code snippets:

```
X = processed_data[["recent_5_year_trend_2_in_death_rates"]]
y = processed_data["age_adjusted_death_rate"]
```

Next, perform a standard train/test split of the dataset whereby 80% of the data is for training and 20% of the dataset is for testing, as performed by the following code snippet:

```
X_train, X_test, y_train, y_test = train_test_split(X, y,
test_size=0.2, random_state=42)
```

The fourth step involves initializing `linear_reg` as an instance of the class `LinearRegression`, after which we can fit this instance to the data. The final portion of Listing 4.3 performs the model evaluation by invoking the `predict()` method of the trained model `linear_reg`. At this point, we can initialize use as the MSE and the R^2 score, respectively, and then print their values. Launch the code in Listing 4.3, and you will see the following output:

```
mse: 145.2243931078172 r2: 0.11141880352501743
```

DESCRIBE THE MODEL DIAGNOSTICS

Model diagnostics play a crucial role in identifying potential issues with the regression model and ensuring the assumptions underlying linear regression are met. Here are the primary diagnostics and associated checks for linear regression:

1. Linearity
2. Independence of errors
3. Homoscedasticity
4. Normality of residuals
5. Multicollinearity
6. Outliers and leverage points
7. Model specification

1. The assumption of linearity means that the relationship between the independent variables and the dependent variable should be linear.

   Diagnostic Tools:
   a. Residual vs. Fitted plot: If there is a pattern in this plot (like a curve), it suggests non-linearity (scatter plots of the observed vs. predicted values).

2. The assumption of independence of errors means that the residuals (errors) should be independent.

   Diagnostic Tools:
   a. Durbin-Watson test: It detects the presence of autocorrelation (a relationship between values separated from each other by a given time lag) in the residuals.

3. The assumption of homoscedasticity means that the variance of the residuals should remain constant across all levels of the independent variable(s).

   Diagnostic Tools:
   a. Residual vs. Fitted plot: If there's a funnel shape, it suggests heteroscedasticity (non-constant variance).
   b. Breusch-Pagan or White tests: These can test for heteroscedasticity statistically.

4. The assumption of normality of residuals means that the residuals should be approximately normally distributed.

   Diagnostic Tools:
   a. Histogram or Kernel Density Plot: For visual inspection of normality.
   b. Q-Q (Quantile-Quantile) plot: If residuals lie on the 45-degree reference line, they are approximately normally distributed.
   c. Shapiro-Wilk test: A formal test for normality.

5. The assumption of multicollinearity means that the independent variables should not be highly correlated with each other.

   Diagnostic Tools:
   a. VIF: A VIF > 10 indicates high multicollinearity.
   b. Correlation matrix or heatmap: For a visual inspection of correlations between variables.

6. Detecting outliers and leverage points is important because outliers can overly influence the model, leading to unreliable estimates.

Diagnostic Tools:
a. Standardized residuals vs. Leverage plot: Helps identify points that have high leverage on the regression line.
b. Cook's Distance: Measures the effect of deleting a given observation.
7. A correct model specification means that there is no omitted variable bias, and no inclusion of unnecessary variables.

Diagnostic Tools:
a. Added Variable (Partial Regression) plots: Helps in checking if a variable adds information to the model.
b. RESET (Regression Specification Error Test): Tests for model misspecification.

For our linear regression model using the `death.csv` dataset, let's conduct some of these diagnostics, starting with checking for linearity, homoscedasticity, and normality of residuals. Based on the diagnostic plots, we have the following information:

• Residual vs. Fitted Plot:
Linearity: There does not seem to be any clear pattern in the residuals against the fitted values, indicating that the linearity assumption is not strongly violated.
Homoscedasticity: The spread of residuals appears to be relatively uniform across the range of fitted values, suggesting that the homoscedasticity assumption is not strongly violated.
• Histogram of Residuals:
The histogram shows the distribution of residuals. While it is not perfectly normal, the distribution does not have extreme deviations from normality.
• Q-Q Plot:
The Q-Q plot shows how well the distribution of residuals aligns with a normal distribution. The residuals largely follow the 45-degree reference line, especially in the center. There are some deviations, especially in the tails, indicating some minor deviations from perfect normality.

To further ensure the model's reliability, additional diagnostics like checking for multicollinearity (more relevant for models with multiple predictors), outliers, and high-leverage points should also be considered. For this simple linear model with only one predictor, multicollinearity is not a concern.

ADDITIONAL MODEL DIAGNOSTICS

The heading for this section was inserted by the author in order to state the purpose of this section, which was not generated by ChatGPT. After prompting ChatGPT to delve deeper into additional model diagnostics for our linear regression, ChatGPT responded with the text shown after the following list of items:

- influence plots
- Cook's distance
- VIF (Variance Inflation Factor)
- condition number

- Influence plots help identify points that have a high influence on the regression equation.
- Cook's distance measures the effect of deleting a given observation. Data points with a large Cook's distance might be influential.
- VIF: While multicollinearity is not a concern for our simple model with one predictor, it is good to be aware of this diagnostic for future reference when you expand the model.
- A high condition number can indicate multicollinearity and potential numerical instability in regression.

Let's start with the influence plots and Cook's distance. Based on the diagnostics, we have the following information:

Influence Plot:
The influence plot provides a visual representation of the observations' influence on the regression. The size of the point is proportional to the Cook's distance, and points further to the right have higher leverage. Most observations are clustered toward the left, indicating low leverage. However, some points, especially those with larger sizes, might be influential.

Cook's Distance:
We have identified 73 observations with a Cook's distance greater than the threshold 4nn4, where nn is the number of observations. These are potentially influential points that might unduly affect the model's fit.

The presence of influential observations suggests a couple of potential courses of action:

Investigate Influential Points:
Before considering removing any data points, it is essential to understand why they might be influential. Are they errors, or do they represent genuine extreme cases?

Robust Regression:
If the dataset has influential points or outliers, consider using robust regression methods that down-weight the influence of outliers.

MORE RECOMMENDATIONS FROM GPT-4

Given the results and diagnostics from the linear regression model using the `death.csv` dataset, here are some recommendations:

1. *Address the Outlier:*

   Investigate the potential outlier identified during diagnostics. Determine if it is a data error or an actual extreme value. If it is an error, correct or remove it. If it is genuine, you can decide whether to keep it, based on the context and its potential impact on the model.

2. *Expand the Model:*

   The current model uses only one predictor. Consider adding other relevant predictors from the dataset to improve the explanatory power of the model. When adding more predictors, watch out for multicollinearity and ensure to run diagnostics again.

3. *Alternative Models:*

   Given the moderate R^2 value, consider using more complex regression models like polynomial regression, ridge or lasso regression, or even non-linear models. Ensemble methods like random forests or gradient boosting machines might also be worth exploring.

4. *Feature Engineering:*

   Explore creating new features or transforming existing ones. For instance, non-linear transformations (e.g., logarithms) might help if certain relationships are not linear.

5. *Handle Missing Values More Strategically:*

   We dropped rows with missing values for simplicity. Depending on the nature of the missing data, consider imputation techniques to utilize more of the data.

6. *Model Validation:*

   Ensure robust validation using techniques like K-fold cross-validation. This provides a more reliable estimate of model performance on unseen data.

7. *Domain Knowledge:*

   Engage domain experts to understand the features better, validate the model's findings, and potentially identify new relevant features.

8. *Model Interpretability:*

   If the goal is to understand the factors affecting death rates, consider using models like decision trees or SHAP values with ensemble methods for better interpretability.

9. *Regular Updates:*

   Depending on how the data evolves over time, the model might need regular updates or fine-tuning. Set up a monitoring mechanism.

10. *Data Quality and Collection:*

    Ensure the quality of the data. If there are systematic errors or biases in data collection, even the best models can produce misleading results.

In conclusion, while the initial linear regression model provides a foundational understanding, there is ample room for improvement and refinement. The best approach would be iterative: refine the model, validate it, interpret results, and adjust as necessary.

SUMMARY

This chapter introduced you to linear regression, along with a description of how to calculate a best fitting line for a dataset of values in the Euclidean plane. You saw how to perform linear regression using NumPy to initialize arrays with data values.

Then you learned how to perform linear regression on the bona fide dataset death.csv, which involved a description of its features.

## CHAPTER 5

VISUALIZATION WITH GENERATIVE AI

This chapter discusses visualization with generative AI, which includes some popular image generation tools that were introduced in 2022 and 2023. You will also learn about AI21 and its playground, along with the Aleph Alpha playground, both of which offer functionality that is similar to the GPT-3 playground. Keep in mind that the Python-based code samples currently require Python 3.7, which you can download from the Internet if you have not already done so.

The first section of this chapter contains an overview of generative AI and some examples of generative AI. Next, you will learn about diffusion, which is a technique for removing noise from an image. You will also learn about diffusion models and how they contrast with GANs (generative adversarial models). This section introduces CLIP and GLIDE, both of which are from OpenAI.

The second section of this chapter contains an overview of several popular tools for text-to-image generation, such as Stability AI, Imagen, Midjourney, and Designer. You will also learn about Make-a-Scene (GAN2), and the differences between GPT-3 and GANs.

The third section delves into images generation, including a brief introduction to the topic of diffusion. You will learn the difference between diffusion models (Imagen and DALL-E 2) and auto generative models (DALL-E). You will also see examples of images that are generated via DALL-E and DALL-E 2.

The fourth section discusses the AI21 playground and the Aleph Alpha playground, using the same prompts that were used for the GPT-3 playground so that you can compare the results (spoiler alert: GPT-3 is noticeably better than these two alternatives).

The third section of this chapter introduces tools for text-to-speech and text-to-video generation, such as Make-a-Video.

The fourth section of this chapter introduces DALL-E 2 and various aspects of this tool, such as the DALL-E 2 model and its tokenizer. You will also see examples in the DALL-E 2 playground, followed by other "playgrounds," such as *playgrounds.ai*.

One important caveat to keep in mind: various companies have policies for their employees regarding the use of AI-based code and the use of AI tools. In some cases, those policies may preclude the use of the AI-generated code in this book - be sure to become acquainted with such policies before you use the code samples in this chapter.

GENERATIVE AI AND ART AND COPYRIGHTS

Generative AI was briefly described in Chapter 1, along with the manner in which it differs from conversational AI. More importantly, generative AI has shown its capabilities in multiple areas, such as films and videos.

One comparison involves the effects of CGI during the 1990s, and its impact on movies from Hollywood. Generative AI transcends CGI in dramatic ways that will result in a disruptive change for multiple industries.

We have already reached the point at which generative AI can create art and even win art contests. The natural question is this: who is the owner of the art? While it might seem fair for AI to obtain a copyright or a patent for its work, a judge ruled that only humans can obtain copyrights for their work:

https://www.reuters.com/legal/ai-generated-art-cannot-receive-copyrights-us-court-says-2023-08-21/

GENERATIVE AI AND GANS

Although Generative AI and GANs (Generative Adversarial Networks) are closely related concepts within the field of machine learning and deep learning, they have differences. Generative AI is a broad term that encompasses any machine learning model designed to generate new data samples. This includes GANs, VAEs, and RBMs.

Both generative AI and GANs have been pivotal in various applications, from image synthesis, data augmentation, style transfer, to drug discovery and more.

Generative AI refers to a broader class of machine learning models that aim to generate new samples similar to the input data. These models learn to capture the underlying distribution of the training data, so they can produce new, synthetic examples that are consistent with the data they have seen.

There are several types of generative AI models, some of which are listed below and followed by brief descriptions:

- Probabilistic Graphical Models
- Variational Autoencoders (VAEs)
- Restricted Boltzmann Machines (RBMs)
- GANs

Probabilistic Graphical Models are statistical models that use a graph to represent and map out the dependencies among various random variables in the data. Examples include Hidden Markov Models and Bayesian Networks.

Variational Autoencoders (VAEs) are neural network architectures that learn to encode and decode data in a way that the encoded representations can be used to generate new, similar data.

Restricted Boltzmann Machines (RBMs) are neural networks with two layers (visible and hidden) that learn a probabilistic model of the input data.

GANs are a type of generative model that uses two neural networks that are called a generator and a discriminator.

GANs (Generative Adversarial Networks)

GANs are a specific type of generative AI introduced by Ian Goodfellow and his collaborators in 2014. They are characterized by their adversarial training process involving a generator and discriminator network.

The unique aspect of GANs is their adversarial training process, which involves two neural networks called a generator and a discriminator.

The generator tries to produce data based on random noise as input and then generates samples as output. The discriminator distinguishes between genuine data (from the training set) and fake data produced by the generator. Here are the steps for the training process:

- The generator tries to produce fake data that looks as real as possible.
- The discriminator tries to get better at distinguishing real data from fake data.
- The process is akin to a forger trying to create a fake painting, while an art detective tries to detect which one is fake. Over time, the forger becomes so skilled at creating paintings that the detective cannot tell real from fake.

Advantages of GANs include the following:

- They can generate very high-quality data, especially images.
- They do not require any explicit modeling of the data distribution.

Challenges with GANs include the following:

- Training can be unstable and sensitive to the choice of hyper parameters.
- They might suffer from mode collapse, where the generator produces limited varieties of samples.

WHAT IS DIFFUSION?

In essence, *diffusion* in generative AI is about simulating a diffusion-like process where data is gradually refined from noise to realistic samples.

The process is inspired by the idea of diffusion, where things spread out and mix over time, but applied in the context of data generation.

Diffusion in the context of generative AI does not refer to the passive movement of particles, as in the physical or biological sense. Instead, it often refers to diffusion models, which are a class of generative models that simulate a diffusion process to generate new data samples.

The following list contains the major aspects of diffusion in generative AI:

- Diffusion models
- Noise-driven process
- Denoting score matching
- Generative process

Diffusion models generate new data samples by simulating a diffusion process. Starting from a random sample, they iteratively refine this sample using a series of noise updates until it becomes a sample from the target data distribution.

The *noise-driven process* refers to the fact that diffusion models add and remove noise to/from data samples. Specifically, start with a real data point and then add noise over a series of steps until it is purely random noise. Next, the generative process involves reversing this noise addition to go from random noise back to a sample resembling the real data.

The denoting score matching refers to the way that a model learns to predict the difference (or "score") between the noisy data and the original data. By learning this score, the model understands how to de-noise the data, which is useful for the generative process.

The generative process step is the inference step that occurs after the model has been trained. In this step, the diffusion model starts with a random noise sample and then iteratively refines this sample using the learned de-noising scores during a sequence of steps. This process gradually transforms the noise into a sample that resembles one of the samples from the target data distribution.

Diffusion models can generate high-quality samples and have been shown to perform competitively with other generative models like GANs and Variational Autoencoders (VAEs). Like other generative models, diffusion models can be used for data generation, image synthesis, in-painting, super-resolution, and other tasks where generating new data samples is required.

Diffusion Image Sample

The following URL is an online application for generating diffusion images from a given image: *https://replicate.com/tommoore515/material_stable_diffusion*.

Figure 5.1 shows the content of `sample3.tiff` that is specified as the input image for the preceding link, and Figure 5.2 shows the generated diffusion image.

FIGURE 5.1: A CSS3-based image

FIGURE 5.2: A diffusion image

The code for this application is available as a GitHub repository:

https://github.com/TomMoore515/material_stable_diffusion

Diffusion Models Versus GANs

According to a paper published by OpenAI in June/2021 with the title "Diffusion Models Beat GANs on Image Synthesis," diffusion models can achieve superior image quality over generative models (along with some limitations): *https://arxiv.org/pdf/2105.05233.pdf*.

The following article discusses GANs versus diffusion models, along with suggestions for how to make a choice between these two options:

https://analyticsindiamag.com/diffusion-models-vs-gans-which-one-to-choose-for-image-synthesis/

What are Diffusers and DDPMs?

Diffusers refers to SOTA diffusion models (written in PyTorch) that are available for more than one modality, such as image as well as audio generation, and the associated Github repository is available at *https://github.com/huggingface/diffusers*.

Denoising Diffusion Probabilistic Models (DDPM) are deep generative models that form the basis for the image generation in DALL-E 2 and Imagen:

https://medium.com/mlearning-ai/enerating-images-with-ddpms-a-pytorch-implementation-cef5a2ba8cb1

CLIP (OPENAI)

CLIP is an acronym for Contrastive Language-Image Pre-training, it is a model developed by OpenAI. While it is not a generative model by itself, it is designed to understand images paired with natural language, bridging the gap between vision and language tasks.

CLIP is a model designed to understand and bridge the gap between vision and language. By learning to associate images with natural language descriptions, it achieves a versatile understanding that can be applied to various tasks, both in vision and in scenarios where it is combined with generative models. CLIP involves the following components:

- Training mechanism
- Contrastive learning
- Zero-shot learning

The *training mechanism* involves a large set of images paired with textual descriptions. The objective is to ensure that an image and its corresponding textual description come closer in the embedded space, while other non-matching pairs are pushed apart.

Contrastive learning is the basis for the training mechanism. In this approach, the model learns to distinguish between positive pairs (correct image-text matches) and negative pairs (random image-text combinations).

Zero-shot learning is a feature whereby CLIP can perform tasks without fine-tuning. Given a set of classes described in natural language, CLIP can classify new images into these classes without requiring task-specific training data for each class.

CLIP can handle a wide range of vision tasks using the same model. This includes image classification, object detection, and even some forms of image generation when paired with other generative models.

Although CLIP is not a generative model, it can be paired with generative models for interesting applications. For example, when combined with a model like VQ-VAE-2 (a generative model), CLIP can be used to guide the generation process using textual descriptions, resulting in a system that can generate images from textual prompts.

CLIP provides robustness because it is less susceptible to adversarial attacks compared to traditional models. CLIP also provides transferability because its understanding of images and text allows CLIP to transfer its knowledge to a wide range of tasks without task-specific fine-tuning.

GLIDE (OPENAI)

GLIDE is an acronym for Guided Language-to-Image Diffusion for Generation and Editing, and it consists of a CLIP embedding plus a diffusion model that compares favorably with DALL-E, even though GLIDE is less than one-third the size of DALL-E.

GLIDE encodes a language prompt by means of a text transformer, and in addition to text, GLIDE can process images that are modified through NLP prompts to insert new objects. GLIDE can also enhance images through various other effects, such as reflections and shadow effects. In fact, GLIDE is preferred by some because of its feature set. The following link provides more details regarding GLIDE:

https://www.marktechpost.com/2021/12/29/openai-introduces-glide-model-for-photorealistic-image-generation/

Now that you have an understanding of CLIP and GLIDE, let's explore some tools that perform text-to-image generation, which is the topic of the next section.

TEXT-TO-IMAGE GENERATION

Text-to-image generation is in the midst of a period of incredible innovation due to the availability of new image generation tools, such as DALL-E, Craiyon, and Stable Diffusion. Other tools are under development, and the race for better feature support continues unabated. Indeed, image generation is experiencing a renaissance that will have a profound impact on artists, designers, and companies that provide graphics-related tools and products.

Along with the success of text-to-image generation, there has been some controversy, such as copyright issues. For example, Getty Images provides a library of almost 500 million images, and it has banned the upload of AI-generated pictures to its image collection because of a concern regarding the legality of such images. Other sites that have implemented a similar ban include Newgrounds and PurplePort. Another contentious incident involved a fine arts competition that awarded a prize to an AI-generated art piece. There is also a growing malaise among artists and people involved in UI graphics regarding the potentially adverse impact of AI-based artwork and design on their careers.

Some image generation tools, such as Craiyon and DALL-E, are accessible via APIs calls or a Web interface, whereas Stable Diffusion is downloadable on your machine. Specifically, the GitHub repository for Stable Diffusion is accessible online:

https://github.com/CompVis/stable-diffusion

Recently there has been a rapid succession of text-to-image generation models, some of which (including DALL-E) are based on GPT-3. In most cases, AI-based techniques for generative art focus on domain-specific functionality, such as image-to-image or text-to-image. Currently, the following models provide the most advanced capabilities with respect to image generation, and they use NLP-based techniques to create highly impressive images:

- Stable Diffusion
- DALL-E 2 (OpenAI)
- Glide (OpenAI)
- Imagen (Google)
- Muse
- Make-a-Scene (Meta)
- Diffuse the Rest
- Latent Diffusion
- DreamBooth (Google)

The DALL-E 2 model was the first of the advanced AI-based image generation models, and it is discussed in a different section later in this chapter.

Stability AI/Stable Diffusion

Stability AI is a for-profit company that collaborated with RunwayML (which is a video editing startup) to create Stable Diffusion, which is an open-source text-to-image generator, and its home page is at *stability.ai*.

Currently, Stable Diffusion has gained precedence over competitors such as DALL-E 2 and Midjourney. Indeed, the open-source community has enabled Stable Diffusion to become the leader (at this point in time) among competing image-to-text models.

The following GitHub repository contains an implementation of text-to-3D Dreamfusion that is based on Stable Diffusion text-to-2D image model:

https://github.com/ashawkey/stable-dreamfusion

The preceding repository contains a Google Colaboratory Jupyter notebook that is accessible online:

https://colab.research.google.com/drive/1MXT3yfOFvO0ooKEfiUUvTKw UkrrlCHpF

The following URLs provide other tools from Stable Diffusion:

https://huggingface.co/spaces/lnyan/stablediffusion-infinity

https://huggingface.co/spaces/sd-concepts-library/stable-diffusion-conceptualizer

https://huggingface.co/spaces/fffiloni/whisper-to-stable-diffusion

Imagen (Google)

Google created Imagen, a text-to-image diffusion model (similar to GLIDE) that also encodes a language prompt by means of a text transformer, and its home page is at *https://imagen.research.google.*

Google researchers determined that generic LLMs, pre-trained on text-only corpora, are very effective in terms of encoding text for image synthesis. Two other noteworthy details: Imagen achieves a SOTA score on the COCO dataset, and humans have ranked Imagen higher than other image generation tools.

The following GitHub repository contains a PyTorch implementation of Imagen that out-performs DALL-E 2: *https://github.com/lucidrains/imagen-pytorch.*

Imagen uses text-based descriptions of scenes to generate high-quality images. More details regarding how Imagen works are accessible at the following URLs:

https://www.reddit.com/r/MachineLearning/comments/viyh17/d_how_imagen_actually_works/

https://www.assemblyai.com/blog/how-imagen-actually-works/

An interesting comparison between DALL-E 2 and Imagen can be found at the following URL:

https://www.linkedin.com/pulse/google-imagen-vs-openai-dalle-2-ritesh-kanjee/

Google also created DrawBench, which is a benchmark for ranking text-to-image models, along with an extensive list of prompts for Imagen:

https://docs.google.com/spreadsheets/d/1y7nAbmR4FREi6npB1u-Bo3GFdwdOPYJc617rBOxIRHY/edit#gid=0

Make-a-Scene (Meta)

Make-A-Scene from Meta provides a multimodal technique that combines natural language and free style sketches to generate representations. Moreover, Make-A-Scene works with input that can be either text or sketches.

In essence, the approach used by Make-A-Scene generates images with finer-grained context, such as position, size, and relationships between objects. Make-A-Scene uses a multi-model approach that combines NLP with free style sketches. Unlike other text-to-image models, Make-A-Scene enables you to provide a sketch that supplements text prompts to generate images.

Diffuse the Rest

Another option is the freely available application "Diffuse the Rest," which is accessible here: *https://huggingface.co/spaces/huggingface/diffuse-the-rest.*

As a simple example, Figure 5.3 shows a manually drawn "stick figure," along with the prompt "alien body," after which the images in Figure 5.4 and Figure 5.5 were generated.

FIGURE 5.3: A stick figure

FIGURE 5.4: A second alien figure

FIGURE 5.5: A third alien figure

GauGAN2 (NVIDIA)

GauGAN2 is an early-stage deep learning model that uses text to generate photorealistic images. Unlike DALL-E 2 (discussed in the next section), GauGAN2 is not based GPT-3, but it is nonetheless capable of combining text with other input types and then generating high-quality images.

Users can type short phrases and then GauGAN2 generates an image that is based on the content of the text. For instance, one "baseline" example from NVIDIA involves a snow-capped mountain range that can be customized to include other features.

PromptBase

PromptBase is another text-to-image generation tool that provides free credits for generating images, and its home page is at *https://promptbase.com/*.

As a simple example, Figure 5.6 shows the image that is generated in response to the following prompt:

```
"Salvador Dali riding a Harley Davidson on Daytona Beach in
Florida and wearing a merry pranksters hat and smoking a
huge cigar"
```

FIGURE 5.6: Salvador Dali on a motorcycle

Limitations of Text-to-Image Models

Text-to-Image (T2I) models have experienced tremendous growth and popularity, and despite their capabilities, there are limitations to what those models can produce, such as generating multiple characters, creating shadows as well as reflections, and the quality of generated text.

If you are interested in this topic, more information is accessible online:

https://arxiv.org/pdf/2208.00005.pdf

TEXT-TO-IMAGE MODELS

Text-to-image synthesis refers to the process of generating realistic and relevant images from textual descriptions. This task is highly challenging due to the inherent complexity of understanding the context, semantics, and nuances within the textual description and then translating that understanding into a visual representation. Over the past few years, deep learning, especially GANs, has shown significant promise in this area.

Important text-to-image models include the following:

- AttnGAN
- StackGAN
- DeepArt

The AttnGAN model uses attention-driven, multi-stage refinement to generate fine-grained images at multiple resolutions from textual descriptions. The attention mechanism allows the model to focus on different parts of the text when generating different parts of the image.

The StackGAN model decomposes the text-to-image generation task into two stages. In the first stage, it generates a low-resolution image from the textual description. In the second stage, it refines the low-resolution image to generate a high-resolution image.

DeepArt is more about style transfer, where a textual description or another image is used to generate an image in a particular artistic style.

The MirrorGAN model leverages the capabilities of semantic text embeddings and the spatial configurations of image scenes to generate images from textual descriptions. It consists of three modules: Semantic Text Embedding, Global-Local Collaborative Attentive module, and a Streamlined Object Generator. You can find open-source text-to-image models from the following locations:

- GitHub
- Model Zoos
- Papers with Code
- TensorFlow Hub

GitHub is the primary resource for open-source projects. You can find implementations of almost all major text-to-image synthesis models, including AttnGAN, StackGAN, and many others.

Model Zoos often accompany deep learning frameworks (such as TensorFlow and PyTorch), and they act as "hubs" where pre-trained models are available. For text-to-image tasks, you might find some models, but GitHub is generally more comprehensive for this specific task.

Papers with Code provides a curated list of machine learning papers along with the code. It is a great resource to find state-of-the-art models and their open-source implementations.

Google's TensorFlow Hub provides reusable machine learning modules. You might find some modules related to text-to-image synthesis, although it is more limited compared to GitHub.

As a reminder, always check the license associated with the code/model whenever you use or build upon open-source models to ensure you are using it in a way that respects the creators' intentions and any associated terms.

THE DALL-E MODELS

Microsoft will add DALL-E to its Office suite and to Azure AI, and Adobe plans to add generative AI tools to Photoshop. Content generator Jasper announced a massive funding round of $125 million.

There are several AI-based image generation models available, and the three models that are discussed in the following subsections are listed here:

- DALL-E
- DALL-E 2
- Craiyon (formerly DALL-E Mini)

DALL-E

DALL-E is an autoregressive model whose name is a hybrid of the name of the famous artist Salvador Dali and WALL-E from Pixar, and its home page is available online:

https://openai.com/DALL-E 2/

DALL-E is a 12-billion parameter variant of the GPT-3 model that performs zero-shot text-to-image generation. DALL-E was trained on a dataset of text–image pairs. You can download the open-source DALL-E project from the following URL:

https://github.com/openai/dall-e

DALL-E uses the GPT architecture to generate pixel-based images from text on a row-by-row basis. Inspired by GPT, it regards the words and pixels as one sequence of tokens and is thus able to continue generating an image from a text prompt.

https://github.com/openai/dalle-2-preview/blob/main/system-card.md

OpenAI has engaged in significant research to block text generation or image generation through DALL-E that contains inappropriate content. DALL-E 2 extends the existing capabilities of DALL-E 1 (e.g., photorealism) and also provides new capabilities beyond DALL-E 1.

DALL-E 3

In late 2023, OpenAI announced DALL-E 3 that was in "research preview." DALL-E 3 is already available for ChatGPT Plus users (which involves a $20/month subscription) as well as Enterprise customers. Moreover, DALL-E 3 will be accessible from an API.

DALL-E 3 is based on ChatGPT, and DALL-E 3 appears to be a significant advance over its predecessor (as well as its competitors). In short, DALL-E 3 is capable of highly detailed image generation that closely reflects the content of your prompts.

As with DALL-E 2, the images created with DALL-E 3 do not have copyrights and you do not need OpenAI's permission to reprint, sell, or merchandise them. Furthermore, users will not be able to generate images that emulate the style of living artists. In fact, DALL-E 3 goes one step further: artists can request that they not be included in future training processes for DALL-E 3. Another restriction pertains to using names of familiar characters.

More information is accessible from the following URL for DALL-E 3, as well as a sample comparison of the image generation via DALL-E 3 and DALL-E 2: *https://openai.com/dall-e-3*.

Paid Accounts for DALL-E

DALL-E initially provided an invitation-only beta program. Several months later, OpenAI made the decision to support paid access to DALL-E, which is designed as follows:

- A prompt for DALL-E will cost one credit.
- Users get 50 free credits during their first month.
- Users get 15 free credits per month for subsequent months.
- Users can purchase 115 credits for $15/month.

Unlike the beta program for DALL-E, users have complete rights to commercialize the images that they create with DALL-E 2, which includes the ability to reprint, sell, and merchandise the generated images. Moreover, users obtain these rights regardless of whether they generated images via a free or paid credit, provided that they follow the content policy and terms of use from OpenAI, which are accessible at the following websites:

https://labs.openai.com/policies/content-policy

https://labs.openai.com/policies/terms

There are some restrictions: OpenAI will reject any uploaded images in DALL-E that resemble explicit material, named content, or realistic faces.

With the preceding points in mind, create a free OpenAI account and then navigate to the following URL to access the DALL-E editor:

https://labs.openai.com/editor

As a simple example, Figure 5.7 shows the generated image in response to the following prompt:

```
Display a Clown in the image of Mona Lisa and the clown
is smoking a cigar and is wearing big sunglasses and is
drinking a beer
```

FIGURE 5.7: A clown smoking a cigar

The following article provides some information about the DALL-E editor:

https://help.openai.com/en/articles/6516417-dall-e-editor-guide

As another example, enter the text "draw an avocado couch" in the text input box, select 4 as "Number of images you want," and click on the "Generate" button. After a couple of minutes, DALL-E will generate four images in response to your prompt, as shown in Figures 5.8-5.11.

Invoking the DALL-E API

OpenAI recently added a public API to access DALL-E. Listing 5.1 displays the content of dalle_api3.py that shows you how to invoke this API and then generate multiple images.

LISTING 5.1: dalle_api3.py

```
# pip3 install openai
import openai
openai.api_key = "your-openai-key"

# a loop to generate multiple images:
basename="avocado_couch"
image_count = 4

for ndx in range(image_count):
  response = openai.Image.create(
    prompt="an avocado couch",
    n=1,
```

```
       # image  sizes  must  be  in  ['256x256',  '512x512',
'1024x1024']
     size="512x512"
   )

   # generate URL with a DALL-E image:
   image_url = response['data'][0]['url']

   # save image:
   import requests
   img_data = requests.get(image_url).content

   filename= basename+str(ndx)+".jpg"
   with open(filename, 'wb') as handler:
   handler.write(img_data)
```

Listing 5.1 starts with an import statement and then initializes open.api_key with your API key. Next, the variables basename and image_count are initialized, followed by a loop that invokes the open.Image.create() method four times (which equals the value of image_count), which then initializes the variable response.

During each iteration through the loop, the variable image_url is populated with the URL by accessing one of the elements of the variable response. The next portion of the loop initializes the variable img_data (which contains the content of the generated image) that is written to the file system of your machine. Notice that the filename for each image depends on the current iteration through the loop. Use this code snippet:

```
filename= basename+str(ndx)+".jpg"
```

Figure 5.8, Figure 5.9, Figure 5.10, and Figure 5.11 display the four images that are generated by the code in Listing 5.1.

FIGURE 5.8: First "avocado couch" design

FIGURE 5.9: Second "avocado couch" design

FIGURE 5.10: Third "avocado couch" design

FIGURE 5.11: Fourth "avocado couch" design

More information about the API is accessible at *https://beta.openai.com/docs/guides/images*.

DALL-E 2

This section is divided into the following subsections that discuss different aspects of DALL-E 2:

- DALL-E 2 Overview
- The DALL-E 2 Model
- DALL-E 2 Content Preparation
- DALL-E 2 and Prompt Design
- DALL-E Tokenizer
- DALL-E 2 and Prompt Design
- DALL-E Tokenizer
- DALL-E 2 Bot

DALL-E 2 Overview

Although DALL-E 2 is a successor to DALL-E, keep in mind that DALL-E 2 is a diffusion-based model (not an autoregressive model such as DALL-E). In fact, DALL-E 2 bears resemblance to GLIDE because both models generate images from a CLIP image encoding. DALL-E 2 uses three main steps:

- leverage CLIP models trained on millions of images
- modified GLIDE model generates images from CLIP embeddings
- diffusion models inject text-related information into images

By way of comparison, DALL-E combines CLIP and diffusion methods to generate photorealistic images using text-based input, whereas DALL-E 2 also includes an "unClip" technique that uses an encoder to process input text. The encoder first generates a representation space that is passed to a model that maps its input to an encoded image, after which a decoder generates the final image.

Furthermore, DALL-E 2 creates superior visual effects compared to its predecessor, such as higher fidelity and more realistic images because DALL-E 2 utilizes more recent SOTA text-to-image techniques. More details of the inner workings of DALL-E 2 can be found online:

https://www.assemblyai.com/blog/how-DALL-E 2-actually-works

In addition to the functionality in DALL-E, DALL-E 2 supports several new features:

- create variations of an existing image
- add objects to an existing image
- edit a selected region of an image
- create an image that blends two input images

Navigate to the home page and register for a free account. Keep in mind one significant difference: any text that you specify and any generated images with DALL-E belong to you for personal as well as commercial use, whereas DALL-E 2 restricts the images for personal use only (i.e., non-commercial use).

In addition to generating images based on text description prompts, DALL-E 2 can modify existing images as via a prompt in the form of a text-based description. Moreover, DALL-E 2 can enhance existing images to create variation of those images (also through text-based prompts).

Another important aspect of DALL-E 2 involves handling inappropriate content. Specifically, DALL-E 2 contains filters that examine user-supplied prompts in an attempt to prevent disparaging, hateful, or harmful content that is directed to individuals or groups of individuals.

In fact, DALLE-2 has mechanisms to block combinations of text or images that are prohibited despite the fact that the individual words or images may be benign. DALL-E 2 also endeavors to detect and block content that suggests gender bias as well as racial stereotypes.

Initial accounts for DALL-E 2 were on an invitation-only basis, which restricted the use of generated images to non-commercial use. However, in mid-2022, OpenAI enabled paid subscriptions for DALL-E 2 that allows commercial use for any images that you create in DALL-E 2 (which makes sense for a paid subscription). According to various articles, there may have been as many as one million people on the initial waiting list for DALL-E 2, all of whom will have an opportunity to sign up for a paid subscription.

In a partially related topic: at least one robot is capable of producing art. Ai-Da (named after Ada Lovelace) is the first robot capable of painting like a human artist. AI algorithms prompt the robot to interrogate, select, and decision-make to create a painting. More information about Ai-Da is in the following article:

https://www.theguardian.com/technology/2022/apr/04/mind-blowing-ai-da-becomes-first-robot-to-paint-like-an-artist

The DALL-E 2 Model

The fundamental components of DALL-E 2 are as follows:

- a CLIP model
- a prior model
- an unCLIP model (decoder)

DALL-E 2 is the result of combining the prior model with the unCLIP model.

- CLIP: Takes image-caption pairs and creates "mental" representations in the form of vectors, called text/image embeddings
- Prior model: Takes a caption/CLIP text embedding and generates CLIP image embeddings

- Decoder Diffusion model (unCLIP): Takes a CLIP image embedding and generates images
- DALL-E 2: Combination of prior + diffusion decoder (unCLIP) models.

DALL-E 2 Content Preparation

OpenAI performed pre-training tasks on the DALL-E 2 dataset to ensure compliance with the content policy of the company, as listed here:

- removal of sexual and violent images
- bias reduction (less filtering)
- removal of repeated images

OpenAI discovered an interesting result: an increase in the amount of image filtering sometimes leads to a more imbalanced dataset (e.g., more men than women). OpenAI also removed repeated images in the training set because of an effect called "image regurgitation" whereby repeated images will sometimes appear in the output instead of generating new images.

OpenAI filtered training data using a technique called GLIDE, which involves the following steps:

- create a specification for the image categories to be labeled
- collect several hundred positive images for each category
- collect several hundred negative images for each category
- use active learning procedure to collect more data

The purpose of the active learning procedure was to improve the precision/recall trade-off. The final step involves applying the classifier on the complete in such a way as to prefer recall instead of precision.

Another important point is that OpenAI focused on the removal of bad data rather than keeping the good data for the following reason: it is easier to fine-tune a model than to make a model "unlearn" something that it learned during the training process.

Navigate to the following URL, where you can obtain more detailed information regarding the combinations of techniques that OpenAI employed to produce a high-quality dataset of images for DALL-E 2:

https://openai.com/blog/DALL-E 2-pre-training-mitigations

DALL-E-Bot

DALL.E-Bot combines a GPT4-based language model with DALL-E, which enables users to specify text-based descriptions from which images are generated. Specifically uses can describe concepts, objects, or scenes as input text, after which DALL-E Bot can generate a variety of images.

In addition, DALL.E-Bot was designed to ensure that the content that it generates conforms to copyrights and does not generate images based on specific individuals. for example, if you specify Pablo Picasso in your input text, DALLE-Bot will not generate images that are based on Pablo Picasso (or any other person from the past 100 years).

DALL-E-Bot can also enable a robot to rearrange objects in a scene by inferring a text description of those objects, generating an image representing a natural, human-like arrangement of those objects, and then physically arranging the objects according to that image.

DALL-E DEMOS

You can test DALL-E and DALL-E 2 by inputting text strings at the following URLs:

https://main-dalle-client-scy6500.endpoint.ainize.ai/

https://gpt3demo.com/apps/openai-dall-e

https://gpt3demo.com/apps/DALL-E 2-by-openai

As a fun example, enter the text "draw a clown car with pineapples" in the text input box, select 4 as "Number of images you want," and click on the "Generate" button. After a couple of minutes DALL-E will generate four images in response to your prompt, as shown in Figure 5.12.

FIGURE 5.12: Four clown cars with pineapples

As another fun example, enter the text "draw an avocado couch" in the text input box, select 4 as "Number of images you want", and click on the Generate button. After a couple of minutes DALL-E will generate four images in response to your prompt, as shown in Figure 5.13.

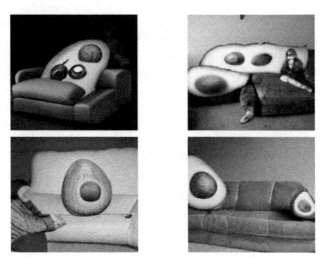

FIGURE 5.13: Four "avocado couch" images generated by DALL-E

TEXT-TO-VIDEO GENERATION

The development of text-to-image tools has been quickly followed by text-to-video generation. Some of the companies that have created text-to-video products are listed here:

- Meta (Make-a-Video)
- Imagen
- Text-to-Video (Stable Diffusion)
- Ruben Villegas and Google (Phenaki)

The products from each of the preceding companies are briefly described in the following subsections.

Meta (Make-a-Video)

Meta created Make-A-Video that performs Text-to-Video (T2V) translation that leverages T2I (text-to-image) in conjunction with unsupervised video content, and currently represents SOTA in T2V with respect to video quality.

One advantage of Make-A-Video is that it does not require paired text-video data. Make-A-Video also has a higher quality of the generated videos with respect to its ability to capture the richness of images from which it generates video-based content. Make-A-Video uses a combination of a U-Net, attention tensors, and a pipeline for creating videos.

Imagen Text-to-Video

Text-to-image models such as DALL-E have an extraordinary capacity for creating awe-inspiring visual effects. By contrast, text-to-video is still in its infancy, probably because this task is much more complex compared to generating images. Nevertheless, Imagen Video from Google is a text-to-video model that relies on diffusion models to produce high-definition videos.

Imagen Video comprises seven sub-models that perform text-conditional video generation, spatial super-resolution, and temporal super-resolution. The result of this process is high definition 1280×768 videos at 24 frames per second. For more information, read the following article:

https://www.marktechpost.com/2022/11/30/google-ai-extends-imagen-to-imagen-video-a-text-to-video-cascaded-diffusion-model-to-generate-high-quality-video-with-strong-temporal-consistency-and-deep-language-understanding/

Ruben Villegas and Google (Phenaki)

Ruben Villegas collaborated with Google to create Phenaki, which is a text-to-video tool that can generate videos that are arbitrarily long. The text itself can have a story-like structure. Examples of videos created via Phenaki are accessible at the following website:

https://phenaki.github.io/

The underlying idea for Phenaki involves treating individual images as if they are frames in a video (which is the true composition of videos). Next, these "videos" are combined with short, captioned videos, which results in long and sophisticated videos by repeating the preceding process. The lower-level details of Phenaki involve the following:

• an encoder that generates video embeddings
• a language model that generates text embeddings
• a bidirectional transformer
• a decoder translates video embeddings into pixels

Note that the bidirectional transformer produces new video embeddings based on the text and existing video embeddings. The resulting Phenaki model is close to 2 billion parameters, which has also been reduced to create a model that is close to 1 billion parameters.

TEXT-TO-SPEECH GENERATION

Generating audio from text has been available as TTS (text-to-speech), and you can find online Python code samples that perform this task. However, some recent AI-based tools can perform text-speech generation to create podcasts. One company that provides this functionality is Play.ht, whose home page is *https://podcast.ai*. One podcast involves Joe Rogan and Steve Jobs, and future podcasts are accessible at *https://podcastio.canny.io/ episode-ideas*.

Whisper (OpenAI)

Whisper is an open-source transformer-based encoder-decoder model that performs multiple tasks, including automatic speech recognition (ASR), multilingual speech recognition, speech translation, and language identification. The audio dataset for Whisper is roughly two-thirds English, and the other one-third consists of data from various other languages. Whisper performs remarkably well for English speech recognition, as described in the following article:

https://openai.com/blog/whisper/

You can also download the Whisper Python-based code from this URL:

https://github.com/openai/whisper

A Google Colaboratory notebook for invoking Whisper functionality is accessible online:

https://colab.research.google.com/github/openai/whisper/blob/master/ notebooks/LibriSpeech.ipynb

Moreover, Whisper has transcribed Twitter videos as well as lectures with an accuracy of more than 99%:

https://twitter.com/ai__pub/status/1574067679555559424

https://medium.com/geekculture/our-knowledge-economy-is-swiftly-coming-to-an-end-734c5dc97355

SUMMARY

This chapter started with an overview of generative AI and some examples of generative AI, and a description of diffusion. Then you learned about popular tools for text-to-image generation, such as Stability AI, Imagen, Midjourney, and Designer.

In addition, you learned about image generation and the difference between diffusion models (Imagen and DALL-E 2) and auto generative models (DALL-E). You will also see examples of images that are generated via DALL-E and DALL-E 2.

Moreover, you learned about the AI21 playground and the Aleph Alpha playground, using the same prompts that were used for the GPT-3 playground. Then you learned about tools for text-to-speech and text-to-video generation, such as Make-a-Video. Finally, you learned about DALL-E 2 and various aspects of this tool, along with a brief introduction to DALL-E 3.

Congratulations! You have reached the end of a fast-paced journey that started with the a brief introduction to Generative AI, mechanism, followed ChatGPT-generated Python code for Python tasks, data visualization, and linear regression, culminating with the wildly popular ChatGPT and GPT-4. At this point you are in a good position to use the knowledge that you acquired as a stepping stone to further your understanding of generative AI.

A
AI21, 9
Akaike Information Criterion (AIC), 101
Anthropic, 9
Apple GPT, 35
Asynchronous programming with Asyncio,
    49–53
AttnGAN model, 136

B
Bar charts, 66
Bard, 33–34
basic_chatbot.py, 44–45
basic_pandas.py, 46–47
basic_visualization.py, 45–46
Box plots, 68

C
ChatGPT
    Advanced Data Analysis, 21–22
        vs. Claude 2, 22
    alternatives to, 27–28
    code generation and handling dangerous
        topics, 24
    Code Whisperer, 22
    competitors, 33–38
    concerns, 23–24
    custom instructions, 17–18
    and data visualization (*see* Data
        visualization)
    generated text, 23
    Google "code red," 16–17

vs. Google search, 17
GPT-3 "on steroids," 16
growth rate, 15
limitations of, 24
machine learning models, 28–29
and medical diagnosis, 19–20
on mobile devices and browsers, 18
playground, 19
plugins, 20–21
probability determination, 58–62
and prompts, 18
and Python (*see* Python)
queries and responses, 25–27
strengths and weaknesses, 24–25
Claude 2, 9, 36
Cohere, 8
Contrastive Language-Image Pre-training
    (CLIP), 130
Counterfactual value-and-policy network
    (CVPN), 7

D
DALL-E, 137
DALL-E 2, 142–144
DALL-E 3, 137–142
DALL-E-Bot, 144–145
DALL-E-Demos, 145–146
Data visualization
    charts and graphs, 65–69
    Matplotlib (*see* Matplotlib)
    Seaborn
        bar charts, 83–84

clustermap, 90–91
facet grids, 89–90
heatmaps, 85–86
histograms, 86–87
joint plots, 92–93
Kernel Density Estimation (KDE)
  plots, 94–95
pairplot() function, 88–89
point plots, 93–94
ridge plots, 95–96
scatter plots, 84–85
swarm plots, 91–92
violin plots, 87–88
vector fields
  polar plots (or radial plots), 83
  quiver plots, 82
  stream plots, 80–82
DeepArt, 136
DeepMind
  AlphaStar and AlphaGo, 6
  history of, 6
  PoG (Player of Games) algorithm, 6–7
Denoising Diffusion Probabilistic Models
  (DDPM), 130

E
Exception handling, 57

F
Few-shot prompts, 11
Fibonacci number using recursion, 48–49
file_handling.py, 43

G
Generative Adversarial Networks (GANs), 2
  advantages of, 127
  challenges with, 127
Generative AI
  art and copyrights, 126
  art and music creation, 2
  challenges, 2
  ChatGPT-3 and GPT-4, 5–6
  vs. conversational AI, 3
    common applications for, 3
    data requirements, 4
    evaluation metrics, 4
    primary objective of, 3
    technologies used, 3
    training and interaction, 4

creation vs. classification, 2
DALL-E, generative characteristics of,
  4–5
data augmentation, 2
diffusion, 127
  denoting score matching, 128
  diffusers and DDPMs, 129–130
  diffusion models, 128
  generative process step, 128
  image sample, 128–129
  models vs. GANs, 129
  noise-driven process, 128
diverse outputs, 2
drug discovery, 3
GANs, 2, 126–127
goals, 1
image synthesis, 3
key features of, 1–2
Probabilistic Graphical Models, 127
Restricted Boltzmann Machines
  (RBMs), 127
RNNs, 2
style transfer, 2
text generation, 3
unsupervised learning, 2
VAEs, 2
Variational Autoencoders (VAEs), 127
GitHub, 136
Google Bard, 27–28
Google's TensorFlow Hub, 136
GPT-4, 31–33
  linear regression
    with dataset, 104–105
    with random data, 101–104
    recommendations, 122–124
  prompt engineering, 14
GPT-5, 38
GPTBot, 18–19
Growing tree CFR (GT-CFR), 7
Guided Language-to-Image Diffusion for
  Generation and Editing (GLIDE),
  131

H
Heat maps, 67
Histograms, 67
Hugging Face
  libraries, 8
  model hub, 8–9

I
Image processing with PIL, 54–57
InflectionAI, 9
InstructGPT, 29–30
Instruction prompts, 11

L
Large Language Model Meta AI 2
  (Llama 2)
  architecture features, 37
  download, 36–37
  fine-tuning, 37–38
Linear regression
  additional model diagnostics, 121–122
  adjusted R², 101
  AIC and BIC, 101
  bivariate and multivariate analyses,
    113–115
  coefficient of determination (R²), 100
  death.csv dataset, 117–119
    detailed EDA on, 110–113
    exploratory analysis, 109–110
    features of, 105–107
    preparation process of, 107–108
  description of, 98
  Durbin-Watson Statistic, 101
  F-statistic, 100
  goal of, 98
  GPT-4
    with dataset, 104–105
    with random data, 101–104
    recommendations, 122–124
  with interaction terms, 99
  MAE, 100
  model diagnostics, 119–121
  model selection process, 115–117
  MSE, 100
  multiple linear regression, 98
  polynomial regression, 99
  RMSE, 100
  RSE, 100
  simple linear regression, 98
  VIF, 101
Line graphs, 67

M
Matplotlib
  box-and-whisker plots, 71–72
  contour plots, 79–80

donut charts, 75
3D surface plots, 75–77
line plots with, 69–70
pie charts, 70–71
radial (or spider) charts, 77–79
stacked bar charts, 73–74
time series data, 72–73
Mean Absolute Error (MAE), 100
Mean and standard deviation, 62
Mean Squared Error (MSE), 98
Med-PaLM M, 35–36
Microsoft CoPilot, 34
MirrorGAN model, 136
Model Zoos, 136

O
Object oriented programming, 49
One-shot prompts, 11
OpenAI
  history of, 7
  instruct models, 7
OpenAI Codex, 35

P
Papers with Code, 136
Pareto charts, 68
Pathways Language Model 2 (PaLM-2), 35
Pi, 28
Pie charts, 66
PoG (Player of Games) algorithm, 6–7
Probabilistic Graphical Models, 127
Prompt engineering
  challenges, 10
  ChatGPT, 13, 14
  and completions, 10
  GPT-3, 13
  GPT-4, 14
  poorly worded prompts, 14–15
  prompt templates, 12–13
  reverse prompts, 11–12
  system prompts *vs.* agent prompts, 12
  types of, 10–12
Python
  asynchronous programming with Asyncio,
    49–53
  basic_chatbot.py, 44–45
  basic_pandas.py, 46–47
  basic_visualization.py, 45–46
  exception handling, 57

Fibonacci number using recursion, 48–49
file_handling.py, 43
generators, 57–58
image processing with PIL, 54–57
random_data_stats.py, 47–48
requests library, 53–54
simple_calculator.py, 42
web_scraping.py, 43–44
Python Imaging Library (PIL), 54

R
Radar charts, 68
random_data_stats.py, 47–48
Recurrent Neural Networks (RNNs), 2
Residual Standard Error (RSE), 100
Restricted Boltzmann Machines
    (RBMs), 127
Root Mean Squared Error (RMSE), 99

S
Seaborn
   bar charts, 83–84
   clustermap, 90–91
   facet grids, 89–90
   heatmaps, 85–86
   histograms, 86–87
   joint plots, 92–93
   Kernel Density Estimation (KDE) plots,
     94–95
   pairplot() function, 88–89
   point plots, 93–94
   ridge plots, 95–96
   scatter plots, 84–85
   swarm plots, 91–92
   violin plots, 87–88
simple_calculator.py, 42
StackGAN model, 136

T
Text-to-image generation
   DALL-E 2 model, 132

Diffuse the Rest, 133–134
GauGAN2, 135
Imagen, 133
issues, 131
Make-A-Scene, 133
PromptBase, 135
Stable Diffusion, 131, 132
Text-to-Image (T2I) models
   AttnGAN model, 136
   challenges, 135–136
   DeepArt, 136
   GitHub, 136
   Google's TensorFlow Hub, 136
   limitations of, 135
   MirrorGAN model, 136
   Model Zoos, 136
   Papers with Code, 136
   StackGAN model, 136
Text-to-speech generation, 147
Text-to-video generation, 146–147
Treemaps, 69

V
Variance Inflation Factor (VIF), 101
Variational Autoencoders (VAEs), 2
VizGPT, 30–31

W
Waterfall charts, 69
web_scraping.py, 43–44
Whisper, 148

Y
YouChat, 28

Z
Zero-shot prompts, 11